GOD MOMENT

Hearing God's Voice Sparks A Remarkable Experience

BETTE & WAYNE PRICE

Contents

1. In the Beginning, God

We were thirty-three years old, committed to each other, proud parents, and living in rural Connecticut.

My father-in-law built our house, and my parents' furniture store afforded me the opportunity to work extra hours to furnish it. I worked hard at several jobs trying to succeed, but nothing felt "right." For me, alcohol became a comfortable refuge.

We were experiencing the typical struggles of a thirteen-year marriage. I wrapped my whole world around pleasing my husband and caring for our girls. However, something was missing. I had a gradual realization that life was altogether flat. I felt at a loss. I was not growing, and I saw no place where I was comfortable. I wondered, "How did life get so stagnant? Is this all there is?"

We became active in Marriage Encounter, where there was talk about the value of God in a marriage. This seemed fine to me as a concept.

Then, among other things, they talked about Jesus, and my best friend was talking about Jesus. However, I prayed to God the Father. I wanted to know how He felt about all of this.
One day the house was quiet, with the girls at school and Wayne at work. I know God heard me when I was just sitting on the sofa and simply prayed,

"Father God, if this Jesus I keep hearing about is so important to You, please show me."

To my amazement He did.

He gave me an immediate desire to find a Bible study.

I thought I overheard that a friend had gone to a Bible study. When I asked her, she didn't know of one but knew of a Catholic church renewal in New York state, just across the Connecticut border. She told me about it briefly, and since I had such a desire to see what God would do, I agreed to go with her. It was totally out of character for me to think of driving not only out of state but also at night and then to a Catholic renewal service when I hadn't been a Catholic since the third grade at St. Peter's school.

I was pleased Bette intended to go out and do something with a friend but surprised when she planned to leave right after dinner and announced it would probably be a late night. However, she was excited and self-assured, so I sent her off with a kiss and my usual admonishments about being careful. I called out, "Have fun!" as she walked down the stairs to our car. I wondered what it was all about, as it seemed very strange to me.

I missed the first night, which was about the love of the Father. The second night they talked at length about Jesus, the Messiah, the Son of the living God, who was crucified for me! With tears streaming down my face, I stood up to receive Jesus as my Lord and Savior when they led us in the prayer of salvation.
They explained the baptism of the Holy Spirit the next night. This time when we entered the church, the

nuns were singing in a foreign language. It did not sound like Latin, but it was the most beautiful heavenly sound I ever heard. Later I realized it was tongues.

> *All of them were filled with the Holy Spirit and began to speak in other tongues as the Spirit enabled them. (Acts 2:4)*

Then on the last night, they spoke about the power of God to heal. Those nights gave me the answer to my simple prayer. I was overjoyed. It was an awesome reality when I truly met the God of the Bible. I know this was God. It was beyond my nature to hear a talk and respond in that way.

This was the beginning, and her whole countenance became brighter. Bette's face was beaming from the first night to the last. Her comments ranged from awe, to trying to explain everything but not being able to, and then to, "You should have been there. Did you want to go?" I politely said no, but I admit I was becoming interested.

I was born again! I hungered and thirsted to know more and was so amazed that God the Father, Jesus the Son, and the Holy Spirit are so real. As I accepted His love, I expected something good to happen wherever I went and in everything I did. I began to read the Bible and looked up words that were new to me in a dictionary. I read the Word with childlike awe. It seemed as though Jesus was close to me at every turn of the page. My life became full of sunshine, joy, peace, and laughter.

When Bette came back from the renewal, I could not miss seeing the difference in her. She was smiling and uncharacteristically talking with her hands while obviously full of joy and at peace. She had books and Bibles scattered

7

all over the house. I complained she was doing it just so I would read them. She said no, and I now believe it was just her way of reaching out to the Lord to receive everything He wanted to give her. Maybe it was just her Bible showing up all over the place, but I could not deny the fact that she had changed for the better, and I wanted it. It wasn't until I saw this change in Bette that I looked for something close to a real God.

I started to attend local prayer and praise meetings. We would all sing of our love for the Lord through joyous worship songs to Him. We would then break into small groups for prayer. At one of these meetings, someone told me about a scripture that says,

> *They replied, 'Believe in the Lord Jesus, and you will be saved—you and your household'" (Acts 16:31).*

I believed and immediately latched onto it. I even asked them to pray over me for my family.

Later when I visited my grandmother, Nana, I talked to her about the Holy Spirit and speaking in a godly language. She was very interested

because she just read a book entitled They Speak with Other Tongues *by John and Elizabeth Sherrill. I enthusiastically offered to take her to her St. Joseph's on Sundays. Since I first met God in a Catholic renewal, I wondered if this was where I should worship.*

However, as soon as communion started, I had a problem. At her church, parishioners walked single file down the aisle to receive the communion wafer from the priest. I refrained from going up to receive it because my upbringing taught it was for Catholics only. I did not want to offend anyone. I loved being with my grandmother, but I stayed in my seat as communion was starting, and when I did not go up to partake, I began to weep. *It got worse every week. Finally, I cried so profusely that I made an appointment to talk with a priest and explained my problem to him. This born-again priest told me there was a little-known new Roman Catholic law that said guests may take communion. Going back to church that next Sunday, I followed my grandmother up and took communion, and there was no more weeping as before. I was surprised, and it taught me the Lord does not want His people to deny Him in order to please man.*

With this resolved, I thought that maybe the Lord wanted me to settle in the Catholic church. Our daughters were going to church with me, and I wanted to get them into a Sunday school class. As a result, I made an appointment, got a different priest, and asked how to do it. He gave a traditional response. He told me the only way it would be possible was to commit to raise my children as Catholic. However, I committed my life to the Lord, not a particular church.

> *Jesus answered, "It is written: 'Worship the Lord your God and serve him only.'" (Luke 4:8)*

In my heart, I still believed my husband would come to the Lord and we would have to make that decision together. This priest quoted a New Testament verse that says,

> *How do you know, wife, whether you will save your husband? (1 Corinthians 7:16a).*

I left saddened since my belief was that the Lord would save my whole house. Therefore, that pathway to a church closed. I believe the Lord was showing me, "No, this is not the way I am leading you." At that time, only our daughter Theresa and I considered ourselves to be saved.

During the time surrounding Bette's salvation experiences, I realized her birthday was coming up. I wanted to get something special, so I decided to get a new Bible for her. She was trying to use the tiny white King James Bible she carried down the aisle when we were married. It was hard for her to read since the type was so small and the translation sometimes used obscure words.

I went to a Christian bookstore and started looking when a salesperson asked if she could help. I made it clear I was not a believer and explained, "It's not for me but for my wife." I asked for the newest, simplest version, which at that time was *The Living Bible*.

This gift was perfect for me. At the time, I needed to know that God and Jesus really loved me. The words in that Bible spoke love to me and were easy to read. It touched me very deeply.

I am sure the salespeople prayed for Wayne after he left because it was obvious he was searching, and I know there were other people praying for him as well. One man from the racquetball club Wayne managed told us afterward he was praying for Wayne but really did not think he would come to the Lord. I am confident God used all of these prayers to prepare Wayne for salvation.

I have had several chances to find God. When I was younger, the kids in the Christian Youth Fellowship at church seemed nicer than at school, so I started hanging out with them as often as I could. My best friend was the preacher's kid, but we never talked about religious things. I gave myself to God earlier, in a junior youth group, but the reality of Christianity didn't take hold simply because the vague preaching and teaching I heard about Jesus had not registered with me.

However, one Christmas season the older youth group was depicting the Nativity scene for the public outside the main entry of the church. When we were finished, we went inside and repeated it for the whole church. I experienced an indelible moment that night when I was up in the balcony running the lights. During a lull in the action, the Spirit of God began to touch me, and I felt a hushed, supernatural peace come over me. I remember nothing seemed important except to experience this deeply quiet time and to be aware of His presence. I said under my breath to God, "Whatever is going on, if You want me, I'm Yours. You can have me." Even with this, I needed to understand in more depth how to be fully His. My revelation of God's presence was still missing Jesus, and reading the Bible was not a part of me yet. Although I accepted the possibility of God, I was not saved; there was no visible change in me.

After my salvation, I searched for as much information about God as I could find. I asked Wayne to tape the Christian 700 Club on TV for me while I was working. I looked forward to listening to those recordings when I came home.

The cassette recorder was on the floor next to the TV. One time as I bent down to turn it off, I heard the host, Pat Robertson, say a word of knowledge that, "Somebody is questioning if God is real." I immediately knew God was talking to me. He then said, "If you will repeat this prayer after me, God will show Himself to you."

I repeated his prayer, saying, "I give myself wholeheartedly to the Lord Jesus. I accept Him and His forgiveness." The host said I could now relate to Jesus as a real and personal God. I made that commitment and received my salvation gladly and quite unexpectedly.

However, in doing so I realized repeating a prayer during a simple TV show would not be satisfying. I needed to know that God is truly real and right around me in order to have a close and personal relationship with Him. I found myself praying surprisingly often and usually on my knees with my youth student Bible at my side. I accepted that this new event happened and went on an immediate quest to prove or disprove it. It was a time of reverent searching for God and reading His Word.

My efforts to find this elusive God took me day after day, and I would say, "Okay, I think You are real, but I crave to hear Your voice. You are Almighty God. Will You speak to me?"

For a long time I heard many voices in my mind, some being my own thoughts, some more authoritative, some more relaxed and easier to hear. Still, I could not absolutely tell for sure which was of God, if any. Soon, He showed me that He does speak clearly and can be easily recognized when He is approached with reverence and true humility.

I was overjoyed when Wayne told me he accepted Jesus as Lord. I saw him seriously pursue God's will in prayer; he did not hold anything back. It floored me to think the Lord and I were moving along at a steady pace and all of a sudden, Wayne was racing ahead in his desire to please the Lord. I had all I could do to keep up with him. I wondered how radical he might become.

The year 1977 was a glorious year when those in our household one by one freely committed their lives to the Lord without pressure from each other. To me that was a definite miracle. I came to Him in March; our nine-year-old daughter Theresa made her youthful decision at an Easter sunrise service. Wayne committed his life to the Lord in October, and our other nine-year-old twin, Wendy, made her early acceptance of Him into her life during a Christmas midnight candlelight service.

Both girls experienced significantly deeper personal revelations of God as they grew into young women.

Another of the precious early moments with the Lord came when our child became ill. One night we were talking in the living room when our daughter came in holding her head. She laid down on the sofa as we realized she was sick and very hot with a fever.

It was late and on the weekend. Our doctor would not be immediately available by phone, and the emergency room was a good distance away.

My husband and I, with the childlike faith of new believers, trusted God without hesitation.–Wendy's was feverish; her head was so hot and dry. She was obviously very sick.

I said, "Well, God heals. Let's go get a Scripture and believe what it says." I found one of the Scriptures in the Bible where Jesus said,

> *"Again, I tell you that if two of you on earth agree about anything you ask for, it will be done for you by my Father in heaven"* (Matthew 18:19).

In another place, the Bible says,

> *"They will place their hands on sick people, and they will get well"* (Mark 16:18b).

We read these Scriptures and decided to believe them. We placed our hands on Wendy and asked the Father to heal her.

It was a simple prayer. We were very young, excited Christians who just believed the words in the Bible exactly as written.

When we laid our hands on Wendy and prayed for her, the fever broke immediately. Perspiration covered her; she laid there quietly and went to sleep. The Lord miraculously and instantly healed her. I carried her into her bed; she slept through the whole night and in the morning was perfectly fine.

God showed Himself strong, and He showed us that nothing is beyond His reach.

Wow! That was such a beautiful moment! The quiet awe that came over us that night was so intense. This was the first healing miracle we experienced. It was simply standing on Bible Scriptures and depending 100 percent on almighty God to provide. We went to bed in wonderment, totally amazed by the reality of what we just witnessed.

2. The Vision

One morning, I was reverently reaching out to God listening to hear His voice.

> *My sheep listen to my voice; I know them, and they follow me. (John 10:27)*

I prayed very often and intently. I was giving all of myself to Him and asking to know His will in our lives. The rarified atmosphere surrounding these prayers was peaceful and calming but at the same time filled with a sense of anticipation. It was very still in the house. I knelt before Him on a small carpet in front of a candle and homemade cross set in the corner of our bedroom and felt the warmth of sunlight streaming into the room.

Suddenly, before me was a vision of a large vehicle with me in the driver's seat. It was so vivid. Even with my eyes closed, I saw it as though I was watching a scene in bright daylight. I clearly saw the inside of the cab and felt the characteristically smooth movement of a large vehicle. It was obviously big, but I did not turn to see the back of it. The cab was not at all like the inside of a truck; it was very open, with two high-backed bucket-style seats. As I looked up, there was something solid and flat overhead, above the visors but below the ceiling. Looking out the windshield, I saw it going uphill and around a right-hand curve. The road dropped off on the left-hand side. The vehicle then seemed to drift off to the left, up, and over a valley. At that point, the vision ended.

I found myself fully awake and still on my knees. As I continued to pray, I asked the Lord, "What did I see? What is this?"

In my mind and between my ears, I heard Him say,

> I want you to buy a motorhome. You will sell your home for fifty-two thousand dollars and buy the motorhome for twenty-six thousand dollars." In addition, the Lord said, "I will send the buyer to you.

It took me the rest of the day to internalize what I experienced. Was this distinguishable voice in my mind really God? It was gentle, authoritative, kind, and very real. The words were certainly not my own. I told Bette about the vision and all of this when she got home from work.

When Wayne shared this with me, a peace came over my heart. I received it with great joy and reverence. Faith filled me with a knowing that this was of God. The certainty of this has stayed with me. I asked many questions, but I knew it was the Lord inviting us to follow Him. But we'd had our house appraised the year before; it was not worth $52,000. However, I knew the Lord would confirm His will as we stepped forward.

Almost immediately, we decided to follow this plan of God. There was never any question of, "Do we believe all of this?" Faith came easily. The next step was to find the vehicle.

The Lord confirmed our little steps of faith as we started to walk out this commitment. First, we needed some additional money to pay our mortgage for the next month. We advertised our little pop-up camper in the

16

classifieds. Some people phoned and said it sounded exactly like what they were looking for; however, they did not show up as promised. Now we were short of the money needed.

I wondered why these people didn't come. Since God is real, shouldn't things work as planned? I started to doubt that I was really hearing God's specific details. However, as I prayed, the Lord said clearly, "Delay is not denial."

My mother knew the would-be buyers and told me later what happened to them; they all came down with the flu. At the end of two weeks, they called and asked if the pop-up was still available. We made the deal that Saturday and were able to pay the mortgage just in time. Consistent touches like this from the Lord helped reinforce the reality of His presence.

We excitedly started looking for motorhomes but in the beginning found only a few small RV dealerships in our area.

Initially our motorhome search proved that new ones were all too expensive, which made us think we had to look for used rigs. While looking in New York State, we saw an old GMC whose cab came the closest to what Wayne saw in the vision. It was an ugly lime green inside and out. At that time, it really did not matter to us because our hearts were fully committed to following the Lord.

Fortunately, when I sat in the driver's seat and carefully looked around the cab, it was not exactly like the vision.

Searching in an ever-increasing area, month after month, we made countless weekend trips to every possible RV dealership we could find.

I read all of the available RV buyers' guides and magazines until I was familiar with just about everything printed on motorhomes. Although our tiring trips netted nothing close to the vision, I wanted to be ready for this expected miracle.

Then a coworker told me about an advertisement from an out-of-the-way RV place that talked about new motorhomes in our price range. We hadn't seen this particular ad, and I was excited about this possible clue to our search. We drove to the outskirts of a small, distant town on a cold, windy September afternoon and found the dealer called A-1.

We walked into the large indoor showroom and saw a Concord brand full-sized RV.

Wayne went directly to the cab, as was our routine. Typically, as soon as he sat down, the girls would ask, "Is this the one?" This time the girls didn't even ask. It had been a long day, and we were all tired.

I sat down, looked out the windshield and exclaimed, "This is like the vision, just exactly! Like the way it looks overhead and the way the visors are!"

We were used to just checking out each motorhome without success. In surprise, Wendy, Theresa, and I said almost simultaneously, "Is it really?"

"Yes, this is the one!"

"We found it!" We found the pearl of great value! We found the one that matched the vision! Thank You, Lord! You are magnificent!

> *Again, the kingdom of heaven is like a merchant looking for fine pearls. When he found one of great value, he went away and sold everything he had and bought it. (Matthew 13:45–46)*

> *Ask and it will be given to you; seek and you will find; knock and the door will be opened to you. For everyone who asks receives; he who seeks finds; and to him who knocks, the door will be opened. (Matthew 7:7–8)*

While we were there, we asked many questions about the motorhome and picked up all the literature they would give us. The Lord said what it would cost, but looking at the sticker prices of short RVs, we found the prices to be somewhat higher.

However, it was close—tantalizingly close. They were the closest sticker prices we had seen up to this point, even used, and it would be a new vehicle. We went away pleased and full of hope.

3. Sell the House

We decided to honor God's words to us during Wayne's vision: "I will send the buyer to you." Therefore, we refrained from getting a Realtor or doing any advertising. Then, acting further in faith, we began selling our possessions. Hope charged the air. We started our tag sales as soon as it was warm enough to put things out in the yard and sold as many lesser-used items as we could, but then it became more difficult. One early sacrificial sale was Wayne's golf clubs and brand new leather bag.

I was glad the clubs were going to someone who appreciated their quality. However, the loss of these prized possessions hit me personally. As the convertible carrying them left the driveway, I even walked a little ways down the road to get one last glimpse of them. I realized selling everything might be harder for me than first imagined.

Following the Lord just became a reality. However, we both found our commitment to be deeper and more certain as the sales continued.

By midsummer, we started selling the bigger items. We put an ad in the paper that included Ethan Allen furniture we bought from the family-owned store, like a sofa, loveseat, dining room table, bedroom set, etc. It created one very large sale. We opened up the house and let people come in to look at the larger furniture.

It was a little overwhelming, as it seemed like twenty-five different people were rummaging through the house all day that Saturday. It was just wave after wave of people. First to go that weekend was our full set of beautiful red pottery dishes and large, round antiqued pine table with four matching captain and mates' chairs. Actually, the dishes were just sitting on the table, and they both sold together. Our daughters were also very much a part of the commitment to sell all and follow the Lord by selling many of their toys and games.

Coffee table books and tools sold easily. Some things went very quickly, like our four-poster bedroom set. We sold everything except the mattress. We just placed it on the floor and slept on it during this season of simple obedience.

It took a long time to get everything sold, but every sale helped us pay the bills for that month. This was a lesson of patience and trust. Even though there was never extra money, we rejoiced in each sale as we saw God's faithful hand to always supply. During that time, we continued to pray in earnest for continued guidance.

We even sold our washer and dryer. Afterward I hand washed and air-dried all of the girls' clothes for school and Bette's clothes for work. This went on for many weeks. Finally, I did go to a Laundromat for a while and told someone we sold our laundry equipment. She asked, surprised, "You had a washer and dryer in your house?" She was amazed we would voluntarily give them up. However, we knew we were following the Lord by selling everything.

The sales continued with many precious God moments taking place. Good friends bought the girls' bunk beds, saying we could keep them until the house sold, and the wife bought a model ship Wayne had built, saying she would sell it back if we ever returned.

As we started to open up about what we were doing, people would ask more about our witness and what the Lord was doing with us. We gladly shared our call from the Lord, expecting a fine reception.

However, our excitement often met raised eyebrows and much advice, most of which was contrary. A few said, "Well maybe the Lord wants you to stay right here."

Nevertheless, we were strongly committed to the Lord's plans for us, as we knew them. We were clearly going to do things His way and not waver. We stayed in faith through many months when little was going on.

While waiting for the Lord to show us our next steps, we were active in the local Methodist church, working closely with several committed believers. We wholeheartedly gave ourselves, as a family, to the ministry of serving other couples and their children. The Lord led Wayne to develop a series of unique games with the goal of encouraging family unity by playing together.

One game consisted of nine large cardboard cubes approximately three feet by three feet by three feet. We wrote a Scripture on one set of sides in a colored marker. Then on another set of sides, we wrote a second Scripture in a different-colored marker. We repeated this on all six sides. Tossing the boxes around jumbled the Scriptures. Initially the kids in one family put the same-colored cube sides facing the group. Then the competing family would quickly move the cubes around until there was one complete scripture showing. The family with the fastest time was the winner.

We also spent time praying for the church body and for individual needs while serving in an intercessory prayer group. Even with all of this activity, we spent a large amount of time just waiting and praying. It became clear that the Lord was teaching patience and giving us time to grow in the knowledge of His ways.

During one of Wayne's times in prayer, the Lord told him to paint the front of the house and the side that faced one particular neighbor. Wayne's dad came over and helped.

We painted the front and then went to the side, but it was late in the afternoon and my father was tiring out. During a food break, I again shared with Dad what the Lord told me about painting the one side. Neither Bette nor I had any clue of why, we were following the Lord's specific directive.

So we painted that side of the house for no obvious reason, but nothing happened. I painted the rest of the house later. Quite a while after this, the Lord said to me in prayer that a neighbor or an agent of theirs would buy our house. We were to prepare for him to come over and eat with us or to share a meal.

I had no idea what we could feed him. That morning I happened to be making granola cereal; it was already in the oven when the phone rang.

It was one of our neighbors asking if his son could come right over to see the house. He asked, "What do you want for the house, fifty-two thousand nine hundred?"

I said, "No, fifty-two thousand even," because it was the exact figure the Lord gave to me. It was an act of obedience, and we looked for confirmation right down to the wire.

When the son came over, he looked at the house. Bette was able to offer him some granola, to which he said, "Sure, I'd love it."

It was a blessing for me to have been led by the Lord to make it that day so I would be able to share it with him right on time.

Then he said, "I'll buy your house." What a glorious God moment! It was a time when God was absolutely in charge.

All the way back at the beginning, the Lord said He would send the buyer to us. In faith, we were determined not to list it with a Realtor or even advertise it in the paper.

> *And without faith it is impossible to please God, because anyone who comes to him must believe that he exists and that he rewards those who earnestly seek him. (Hebrews 11:6)*

Up until that time, we did not know the neighbor had a grown son or that he was even interested in buying a house. When we were doing our yard sales, we mentioned the price of the house to his father. We thought maybe we could sell it to a neighbor, but neither of them showed any interest at all. The son worked on oil rigs in the North Sea and had just come home. As he talked with us, we found that he recently decided he had had more than enough of that kind of work.

These events proved that it was God speaking all along! It was this son, who had just come home, who bought the house! Of course, his dad was the neighbor who lived on the side of our house the Lord told me to paint! In addition, this happened right after Bette had granola in the oven! This amazing God moment occurred that morning just the way the Lord promised two years before!

It took quite a while to reach this point, but we needed that much time to grow in faith, to trust the Lord, and to be ready for how quickly the days were about to fly by. However, when we ran out of possessions to sell, our income was insufficient to keep up with mortgage payments.

We were several months behind at that point and out of time with the bank since their patience had worn thin. They were threatening foreclosure.

Then the breakthrough happened. The house was almost ready to occupy, and the buyer wanted to move in as soon as possible. We met the legal and bank needs within just a few days since the Lord provided an amazingly quick closing! Praise God, for He is neither early nor late but always right on time!

The Lord's timing was flawless. All we needed to do was stand firm in faith and not give up. The Lord showed He is able to pull out a powerful victory even when things seem to be out of control to the natural eye.

4. The Motorhome

During the process of selling everything, much time passed between our trips to the A-1 dealership. In the beginning, we were there once or twice a month. At home while we waited for a buyer, we pored over the drawings, pictures, and choices, finally settling on the size, floor plan, options, and details we really wanted and believed the Lord would provide. We went back numerous times after that. Finally, on the last trip, the owner said to us, "We have nothing more to tell you until you are ready to order." We went back so many times because we wanted to keep the vision's hope alive and right in front of us. We actually hoped to go one more time but did not have enough money to put gas in the car, and A-1 was a two-hour drive away.

One Sunday after church, we were all sitting around in the living room. The house was very empty; there was one recliner, a borrowed card table and chairs, our mattress, and the girls' beds. We all committed to the Lord that we would go and serve Him even if we had to live in a tent. I had my Bible open, and we began to pray, just to spend time together, the Lord and the four of us. As I read, I thought I saw a Scripture about A-1, but actually it was about Ai. The words popped off the page:

> *Then the Lord said to Joshua, "Do not be afraid; do not be discouraged. Take the whole army with you, and go up and attack Ai. For I have delivered into your*

hands the King of Ai, his people, his city and his land. (Joshua 8:1)

We received this Scripture as an encouragement from the Lord. We prayed and agreed we would go to A-1 the following weekend after I received my next paycheck. We had a Scripture to stand on for encouragement, but we had to wait.

I wanted to break the disappointment and prayed. Though we did not have enough money to go to a fast-food restaurant, the Lord reminded me that I saw a newspaper article stating McDonalds was taking old eyeglasses and giving them to less-fortunate people in developing countries. For every pair of glasses brought in, they would give a free hamburger. We looked and found six pairs of glasses.

We were grateful and had fun enjoying our feast. The following Sunday all four of us went to A-1.

When we got there, we were just wandering around looking at motorhomes, slide-in truck campers, tents, pop-ups, and everything else in the showroom.

They ignored us, which was fine because we did not want their attention. We just wanted to touch our dream again—the God-given vision. We went back home refreshed and waited on the Lord.

Several months later, after collecting $26,000 from the closing of our house and temporarily living with Wayne's folks, we went to A-1 with the intention of putting in an order. We were now ready. A salesman asked, "Can I help you?"

I said, "We know what we want." I explained the details to him. He wanted to know what price we were willing to pay. I said, "Twenty-six thousand dollars."

He responded by saying, "Well, it's never going to come down that low. The cheapest one I have is thirty-nine thousand dollars."

We asked to see the owner who worked so closely with us, but they said he recently died. In addition, it was a new model year, and as a result, all the prices were now higher. And despite the higher price, the one they had was short and much too small for us. We left disheartened.

A few days later, while I was thinking about what we should do next, my mother suddenly yelled down the stairs. "Somebody wants to talk to you. They are on the phone." It was someone from A-1, who said, "Hey, a factory is being closed down, and we just got the right to buy a demo motorhome from last year. It is thirty-two feet long and is loaded. Do you want it?"

I asked, "What's the price?"

He said, "I think we can do it for the price you need."

I responded, "Yes, I'm sure we want it, but I have to phone my wife and have her agreement."

He said, "Well do it quickly because this thing is going to go fast, and I have to call them right back."

I called Bette at work, relayed what had just transpired, and asked, "What do you think about it?"

I felt faith and hope rising again. The Lord was putting victory back in our grasp! I felt a burst of joy welling up. It was in our price range! How could I say no?
"Well, I think so, but can we go see it?"

"No, we have to make the decision today."

"What do you think?"

"I think it's ours. I think we should take it." Bette agreed. I called back and declared, "We will take it!"

We only stayed at my parents' house for maybe two weeks. I don't think it was even that long. We had just closed on the house. We had the money and very quickly agreed to buy a motorhome sight unseen. With just a few descriptions, we committed to take it. They needed to order it that day and give the okay for the factory to drive it right out.

I was thrilled that the vehicle I saw in the vision so long ago was really going to be ours. The house sold just the way the Lord spoke to me, and now the rig was coming too! A sense of reverential awe flooded over me. Both excitement and peace were mine as I sat down and reflected over these amazing events.

In our early exuberance, we went to see a Concord factory near Oneida Lake in New York and were able to see a motorhome on the assembly line. We saw how the motors were just sitting on the frames, and then how they built the coach up from there. This same factory was the one that shut down and had the demo. This was another moment of confirmation that the Lord was running this whole thing; He held that demo for us until our faith was tested.

The price was exactly what the Lord gave us! We bought it for $26,000 after everything, taxes, title, and all the rest! When we went to pick it up, it was in the shop. They were doing the last-minute things a dealer has to do to get a vehicle ready.

We were able to sit in the rig for a few minutes but could not sit in the cab while they worked inside. However, as Bette and I sat in the dinette, I asked, "Can you live in this?" She smiled back and joyfully said, "Yes."

We stepped out and waited for them to finish. It was late in the day, and they were anxious to leave. Finally, they completed their work and prepared to give it to us.

While we waited we saw a current-year Concord in the showroom, and Wayne sat in that cab again.

It was not like the one in the vision the Lord showed me so many years before. I had doubts. I was not sure it was going to be right.

They parked the motorhome in the parking lot when it was finally ready for us to take possession. When I sat in the cab, I was relieved to find it looked precisely the same as in the vision. We looked around at it briefly, but it was getting dark and we wanted to go. I started it up and drove away, with the girls in the back watching Bette as she followed us in the Pinto.

The dealer said they fueled it up. However, as we were driving down the road, I noticed there was not enough gas in the main tank to get us all the way home. I switched over to the auxiliary tank, and the engine died. I tried to start it again on this second tank, which they said also had fuel in it, to no avail. I switched back to the main tank, and it started right up. Then we went to a gas station that was right in front of us. We filled up and drove back to the dealership quickly, but they were just locking the doors. I told them about the problem, and they said there probably was not enough gas in the second tank because everything else worked. The shop men were gone, which meant there wasn't anyone available to look at it, so we left with what we thought was a minor problem and drove it home.

The Lord was so fully with us during this whole process. As I followed behind the motorhome, I saw it was solid and stable on the road. I rejoiced in the awesomeness of His faithfulness and great power.

The Lord showed His intimate involvement with us by selling the house exactly the way He said it would and then providing a motorhome that was precisely the same as in the vision and for exactly the right price!

It had everything on our rather extensive dream list including some details that only the Lord would know about.

It came with two air conditioners, a generator, and a split bath. It also had a two-door exterior, a slide-out pantry, and tambour cabinet doors. It had an upgraded interior, with twin beds in the back for our daughters and a pull-down over-cab bed that we could have slept on. Later I converted it into a queen-sized bed area that slid out into the living room at night. It became a big, comfortable sleeping room for us that was far enough away from the girls for privacy. This rig was outstanding for the price!

> *And we know that in all things God works for the good of those who love him, who have been called according to his purpose. (Romans 8:28)*

It was proof enough for us that the God of the Bible is indeed very real.

5. Up on Shelving

We arrived back at my parents' house late that night. They agreed to let us put the motorhome in their side yard, but we could not get it up the steep entry into their driveway. The back end of the rig continually hit the pavement no matter how we approached it; the slope of the driveway was just too severe. They lived halfway up a very hilly road, so the only place to park was at the top and on the side of this narrow, busy country lane. The motorhome was not safe to leave there for any length of time.

The next morning was clear and sunny, so we decided to try backing it up on shelving that Dad owned. We supported the shelving on rocks we got from their stone wall. We assumed we could raise the rear high enough to clear.

Wayne drove it, and his dad helped the best he could. I was at the side, and Wayne asked me to yell out what was happening. It all looked perilous to me, but I kept my opinion to myself and prayed fervently.

We backed the rig up on this fragile ramp. The rocks were crumbling and Bette was holding her breath and praying, but we finally reached the top.

The Lord mightily protected us in this naïve effort, and I was amazed we got it up next to the house. I saw it as being a miraculous moment. However, the thrill of this victory lasted only until we realized the next problem. How would we get it back down?

The next Sunday at church, our good friend Charlie, who knew of our problem said, "I've been thinking and praying about that. What about railroad ties?" I didn't know anything about them, but he insisted I look because he thought they would work. We drove to the lumberyard. There were landscape ties, which were too small, and then there were actual railroad ties that were larger, heavier, and obviously more stable. We went up, measured the driveway, and looked at what we needed to do.

I bought the ties; we went back up to the house and dumped those heavy square logs on the side of the driveway. After making all of the preparations, including cutting down the ends to make ramps, we tried the system cautiously. It worked perfectly. The ties lifted the back of the rig just high enough to clear the hitch. Every time we needed propane or to dump wastewater, we were able to take the rig out. However, I knew this would not work long term. It soon became clear we could not live in it comfortably full time if we needed to set up and take down the ties every time we wanted to go in and out of the driveway. I could do it, but the ties were difficult for one person to move.

Wayne found a job in the classifieds working at an RV dealership. Although they dealt primarily with pop-ups and travel trailers, he was able to learn a great deal about RVs in general and their onboard systems. He traded some of his time to buy what we needed.

Through this work, and by reading tech articles in a few magazines, I learned how to make the rig work while parked semi permanently. I bought two thirty-gallon propane tanks that could be used and refilled repeatedly and mounted them under the rig. We also bought a necessary extra fresh water tank to increase our capacity. Finally, we purchased a macerator pump that dumped the wastewater through a large garden hose and into an infrequently used toilet. All of these improvements made us able to live comfortably without moving.

At this time, we did not have any idea of how long we needed to stay in Connecticut. The only thing the Lord told us was,

> You will leave when the price of gasoline goes down at your regular station.

This seemed so far away since the prices were regularly rising. When would this motorhome actually travel down the road, and besides, where were we supposed to go?

The answer to half of this question appeared ten months later, when my father came home from work and surprised us by saying, "It looks like the price of gasoline has just gone down." We praised and thanked the Lord when the next day we looked and found they had indeed dropped to $1.19 a gallon. These types of events continually confirmed the words of the Lord as recorded in my prayer journals.

Our excitement was palpable as actual plans for being on the road filled our minds. I gave my notice at work that put action to our faith. The actual duties to prepare for going on the road were many but seemed to go quickly as they became our focus. Leaving the safe environment of friends, family, familiar stores, the church, and jobs was unsettling, but the challenge of a new start filled us with hope. However, we wondered what it would all be like since we hadn't lived apart from our shore connections for any length of time. We installed several new systems and repaired some existing ones. Would everything work as planned?
On July 20, the Lord spoke a date to leave. He said,

Try to be ready by Monday, August 4.

We finished the last of the details. At our going-away party on Saturday night, August 2, friends asked what we still needed to sell before we could go. Along with our car, we mentioned the living room carpet and the girls' bikes. One of the mothers at the party said her thirteen-year-old son would buy the bikes; he renewed and then resold them. Another couple said they would buy the carpeting.

We received our sendoff gratefully. However, as we got ready to leave Connecticut, our little Pinto car was the last possession to be sold. We cringed hearing the nightly news announcing a major recall on Pintos because some of their fuel tanks exploded when rear-ended. We prayed about this because we needed the sale to provide money to go with. The Lord nudged us to continue trying to sell it.

We placed the clear words of the Lord onto a classified ad, saying, "Price firm." The only thing that was firm was the amount of money the Lord said we needed, not the value of the car.

My mother phoned us at the going-away party with name and number of someone answering our ad. I called and set up a time for him to see the car the next day, Sunday, August 3. He checked the car out and said he would take it. He liked the words *price firm* because he did not want to argue over money. Praise God!

The following day, August 4, we met his wife at their bank, exchanged the car for cash, said good-bye to Mom, and drove away in the motorhome. Each one of these events is a treasured God moment. He met us faithfully as we continued to step out with Him.

6. The PTL Campground

Our day was hectic with activity as we prepared to leave; the departure took longer than expected. A very short trip to a park-like rest area at exit 1, I-84 on the Connecticut/New York border was as far as we could travel that first night.

Now that we were finally on the launching pad, the anxiety of leaving what we had known all our lives gave me great insecurity. We were on our way but had no specific direction from the Lord of where to go or what to do next. I felt vulnerable embarking on this new and uncertain quest.

With the girls resting quietly in their room, the two of us contemplated our future in the stillness of the motorhome. I was excited, Bette pensive. A storm brewed outside, but the Lord's peaceful presence was inside.

The drenching rains let up just as I looked out a window and realized I could see a vivid triple rainbow. Stepping outside into the cool, moist air, we all looked up and saw this beautiful, brilliant sight up against the charcoal grey sky.

It was memorable to me, and I interpreted it to mean the three bows represented His ongoing favor over each of our girls and us. It was a significant moment to me in that it convinced my heart the Lord was with us as He was with Noah. The Lord knew and met my need for assurance before I would be comfortable moving forward. I kept this moment deep in my heart.

Prior to this time, Bette and I thought traveling into the warm Southern states and maybe going to the beaches would be nice, but I did not know if the Lord would agree. Kneeling in prayer, with maps spread around me, I asked if we should go north, south, or west. I was unsettled, looking for details like where to make our next night's destination. I hoped the Lord would plan everything out for me; I wanted Him to give me something sure to grab onto. I waited for an answer. God spoke, but not in the way I thought:

> Wayne, Wayne, Wayne. You told everyone you saw that you did not know where you were going or what route you would be traveling, but now you prepare to leave and you do not trust Me? You chose to go south, and that is fine by Me. You see the road that seems best, and that is also fine by Me. But now you don't have a stop planned and so you have questions? Come to Me! I am your refuge! You have more travel books and money and supplies and communications than most of My people. But you also have more security...you have Me! If you travel in praise and trust, then you will ask Me for a place to rest, and I shall provide one. Or you will ask for strength to continue on, and that shall be provided—just as it has always been! You have

learned that I am trustworthy; I still am!

We did decide to go south and see the ministry of Pat Robertson in Virginia Beach, Virginia. We would go see if they could use our help and try to find a job.

The television studio was impressive as we arrived in time to watch a live *700 Club* program. Afterward we looked around briefly and found it to be pleasant and well run. However, we did not feel led to stay and truly sensed we did not belong. We did not try to find the employment office or even look further.

In addition, we were not at peace in the nearby campground located in the Back Bay area. It may have simply been a pervasive negative attitude in everyone we encountered there, but the heavy and wearisome air was oppressive. I went for a walk and returned saying, "We have to leave; this place feels evil."

We were unprepared for this atmosphere having lived a rather sheltered life in Connecticut. Wayne and I were in disagreement over what to do next, with both of us being surprised at the level of our discomfort.

Bette was especially unsettled and fell headlong into fear that made things even worse. We agreed to drive farther south, so we left very early the next morning. We felt an immediate freedom.

I remembered there was a campground at the PTL ministry in North Carolina. We made the trip in one day but arrived late at night. At daybreak, we found we were in a comfortable campground within a large Christian TV–based complex. Deciding we would like to stay longer than a few weeks, Wayne applied for work in the ministry; actually, he was looking for any full-time position. The personnel office told him there was nothing except possibly a part-time waiter job at the restaurant. However, this time we sensed peace in our desire to stay and believed there was more here for us. We rekindled our total reliance on the Lord.

I spent most of the following Sunday in open-ended time with the Lord. This time these prayers did give me specific guidance to resolve the critical issues. He solved my need to find work when I found a measure of faith rising in me. I assuredly walked into the general store and applied directly there. A shift supervisor job happened to open up that day! They hired me on the spot. It amazed me that the Lord was so timely. The request to fill this position never even reached the personnel office!

But now, how would we survive without enough money for the next two weeks? The Lord also spoke clearly about how to handle this problem. He guided us through getting a small loan but said I must produce enough money to pay it off in one month. He explained how extra hours might do this, but I had to know exactly how much would be available. Later prayers revealed the amount of the loan, what it was to be used for, what to buy and when, a way to prove our financial strength after leaving Connecticut, and other incredible details. Only the Lord could have walked us through this maze of needs and the ones that piled up around the same time.

We surprised ourselves with how much help we needed from God just to put the steps of doing things in order. The Lord was so close and provided the answers to specific questions as well as assurances that we would accomplish all of this easily. We were able to borrow the $250 we needed from the bank without even providing a paystub, due entirely to the power of God. He worked it out so the due date to repay would be four weeks away. The repayment from overtime happened exactly one month later, just as the Lord required. We gratefully used *this money to buy simple things like food and the site fee for two weeks in advance. This took more than half of the loan. It was amazing to me that there was ever enough money since Wayne only made $3.67 per hour! His first regular paycheck was just in time to cover the next campsite fee and keep us going.*

There were so many moments like this, when things happened just in time. The Lord was so intimately involved in meeting all of our specific life hassles that we continually thanked Him for His faithfulness.

Another example of a God moment was the same afternoon when we were in Charlotte buying our usual groceries. Then we went to a health food outlet to purchase an inexpensive fifty-pound bag of soybeans. As a result, we drove farther than expected, ending up on the outskirts of the city.

We had done our shopping and headed back to PTL to get Wayne ready for work the next morning.

We were moving quickly on a busy four-lane beltway, and the rig hesitated. We were out of gas in the main tank, so I switched to the auxiliary tank. The engine died, just as it had when we bought the motorhome from A-1. This time it was right in an active lane of the highway.

It was dark, we were in the middle of the highway, and I quietly started calling out to the Lord in prayer.

> *"And call upon me in the day of trouble; I will deliver you, and you will honor me" (Psalm 50:15).*

Wayne knew he could not fix it on the road, so he got on the CB radio and called for help. We got a towing company dispatcher, who wanted to know where we were. We did not have a map of the city or anything to help. There were no mile markers we could see, no exits signs, and no remarkable landmarks near us. Cars were rapidly changing lanes around us, blaring horns, and speeding by, just barely avoiding certain collision.

I put out a call to anybody listening on the CB emergency channel nineteen, asking if someone could tell us where we were. I gave out just what we could see, like a church and a large curve in the road. We knew what main route we were on, but that was it. Many people on the radio tried to help, to no avail, until one man who was driving by saw us and said, "I've got the motorhome." He told us where we were.

I contacted the dispatcher again and this time talked directly to the tow truck driver, who asked if we had cash. I said yes, but of course, we were right at the end of our resources. We agreed to have him tow us to a Sears's auto repair place up the road a little ways. After he disconnected us from his truck, he said, "You're lucky it's a newer rig." He previously decided that if it was a "big, old, broken-down motorhome," he was not going to tow us. Another God moment occurred when he asked for just forty dollars. I paid him with the last of the bills in my wallet without touching the money needed to stay at PTL.

Now, however, we sat stranded in a parking lot; Sears had already closed. We found we were totally in faith, relying on the goodness of the Lord. I was praying in tongues, believing that somehow He was going to get us through this. Wayne tested and checked things out under the motorhome. I was amazed at all the things he was doing, including siphoning gas from the line by mouth to see if it was blocked. It was not. Nothing was successful. Wayne came back inside the motorhome, and as both of us were praying, he received an image of the fuse block and a thought, clearly from God, to check it out.

48

It seemed unnecessary since the dealer checked the fuses, but in obedience, I opened up the panel. A fuse was missing but labeled as fog lamps we did not have. Up to now, I never noticed an extra wire wrapped around one end of that fuse holder. There was no hint that would explain the purpose of this innocent-looking little wire. Holding the wire in its jury-rigged place, I installed another fuse to connect it firmly. After doing so, I heard a solenoid click under the rig. I tried the engine, and it started right up.

Apparently, the missing fuse and this little red wire worked to run the auxiliary gas tank. Thank You, Jesus, for instructing Wayne on what to check and for providing one more example of a God moment!

We arrived back at our campsite at midnight with no further problems. We slept in awe, realizing the Lord made it possible to get back in time for an important day at the store. Again, the Lord tested our faith right up to the last minute, but He was always right with us and perfectly on time.

Back to soybeans. The reason we bought them in Charlotte is when we were at the 700 Club bookstore, we bought and read Pat and Dede Robertson's book Shout It from the Housetops *that talks about the protein in soybeans. When they first started out in ministry with little money, they ate soybeans. He and his wife had a few recipes that inspired me. I cooked the soybeans in a large crockpot and ground them into a meal used to mix into all kinds of food.*

In Connecticut, I found you could buy meat ends inexpensively from a deli. They are meat and cheese loaf pieces that are too small to cut and sell, but Bette and I could still get plenty of protein out of them.

The first dinner I made from the deli ends and whole beans was a tasty baked bean and ham dinner. After that, I mixed the meal with some chicken or just a little ground beef and put it into casseroles. With the Lord's guidance and creativity, I was able to stretch our food far enough that we were able to share with others. I learned to bake nutritious bread and big muffins that got rave reviews. I also combined the soy meal into a breakfast coffee cake with honey and dried apricots.

We bought dried fruit in the bulk food section of Kroger's so it was as cheap as we could get it. We were also able to purchase large, inexpensive tin containers of local honey that Bette used in her cooking and baking. The Lord continually helped us find ways to save on food expenses.

We ate better with the Lord during those days than we did back when we had more money. During that year, the entire family enjoyed very nutritious food with great thankfulness for the Lord's provision. I was able to get our food budget down to fifty dollars a week for our family of four.

The girls became used to the soybean meals, and they were as pleased as I was with the quality of our food. Bette also picked wild strawberries in the spring and incorporated them into the food supply.

During these times, we were at a very deep level of peace in the Lord. We had great confidence and joy in just being with Him daily.

Early one morning the man next door went outside and yelled at the top of his rather raspy voice, *"Praise the Lord!"*

At first, we were confused about what was going on because we could not hear the words clearly. Soon we discovered he was simply declaring his joy over knowing the Lord.

Bette made some food for this neighbor, producing a soy casserole with a little chicken. He received it gratefully and ate it all!

It was a blessing to be able to share it with him. I tried to share dinner with a neighborhood girl whose parents were late getting home. That night our meal consisted of another soybean casserole. Naturally, she hadn't acquired a taste for it. We all chuckled after she left because to us soy was like manna, and we were so grateful for it.

I totaled up what we needed for tithes, campsite, food, propane, gas and miscellaneous items and figured we needed about $12,000 for the year. When I did the taxes the next spring, I found our income was actually just a few hundred dollars above $12,000. This was again a beautiful moment confirming that the Lord is intimately interested in the welfare of His people.

My joy was full living and working for Him. I remember walking home from the store, seeing the motorhome in the moonlight, and remarking to the Lord what a great blessing it was to have that beautiful rig, that we lived in it, and I had a job serving His people. The Lord blessed us with many moments confirming the correctness of us being in that place at that time.

One night when Wayne came home, he told me about his walk to work that afternoon. He was walking down our road, which curved around a small lake, and he suddenly saw a full-sized mountain lion on a hill above him. I asked him, "What did you do?"

I stopped, looked at this large animal, and said, "Looky here!" We both froze and stared at each other. Finally, the big cat turned and went back up and over the hill. I continued on to the store, being just a bit more aware that our site was nestled in some rather deep woods.

The Lord obviously protected Wayne. I knew I would not have been that calm. I am glad I heard about it after the fact!

I found the site particularly quiet and peaceful. Our neighbors, most of whom worked in the ministry in some capacity, always spoke about God whenever we met. Everyone felt the noticeable energy of PTL and shared freely.

The Lord drew me into His presence as I observed His handiwork all around our secluded end of the campground. Walking near our site in the spring, I looked up and saw a canopy of blooming tulip trees at least a hundred feet high. As the evening grew dim, I could hear owls hooting in the warm night air, as well as music coming from the brightly lit outdoor amphitheater not far away.

This was a great time for our girls too. They were able to ride the tram, which traversed the entire complex, have some freedom from us, and do their own ministry with the people who came to visit PTL. They chatted with the guests, answered their questions, and helped them find places they wanted to see on those sprawling grounds.

It was a blessed time for them. Wayne and I were also at peace with this because the campground had security guards who came to know our daughters and kept an eye on them as they moved about.

The store issued Wayne a uniform of jacket, slacks, shirts, and ties. We even found that to be a great blessing since he preferred to wear dress clothes at work. With eyes totally on the Lord, we thanked Him for each blessing, including the small ones. This kept our joy full. During our year at PTL, we experienced our significant moments by truly seeking God and having personal and intimate involvements with Him.

This year was great, but in the next, we found a completely new set of challenges in a very different world.

7. Then God Said, "Aspen"

One weekend we decided to get away to a campground with a small lake in the mountains of western North Carolina. On the return trip, we stopped at a scenic viewpoint where a sheer vertical rock outcropping was exposed. Stairs lead directly up next to the face of it. The girls wanted to go explore ahead of us. Bette wanted to stay behind and prepare lunch, I went outside to go for a walk. I basked in the presence of the Lord and just enjoyed the day.

Unexpectedly, the Lord said to me quietly and clearly, "I want you to move to Aspen." I was surprised He wanted us to go there, but the thought of another move was exhilarating. I did not wait around to hear more, like what we were supposed to do there.

I simply said to the Lord, "The girls are never going to want to move from the Carolinas. They have their friends here." Besides, I thought to myself, *We are settled and part of a Christian ministry. What could Aspen have to offer?*

However, He told me the girls would want to go, if for no other reason than just for the skiing. Although I was still unsure, I went back to the motorhome. I told Bette what I heard the Lord say and about the girls wanting to go.

I knew Wayne intended to use the girls' responses as a Gideon-type fleece (Judges 6:37–40) to see if he was hearing the Lord accurately. He really did not think the girls would want to go. I felt confident that when Wayne said he heard from the Lord, it was true.

I went a little ways up the side of the mountain to be with the girls. When we came back down and were all in the motorhome, I told the girls what the Lord said. Their immediate response was, "Fantastic! Great! When do we leave?"

I knew the girls were happy but did not expect them to want to move so readily. I received all of this with faith, but my first thought was, "Where is Aspen?" Wayne picked up the road atlas. In the beginning, we didn't even know where it was in Colorado, but upon finding it on the map, it looked very small and out of the way.

When we got back home, the words of the Lord continued to blossom. During my prayer times, I continued to hear "Aspen" many times throughout our last month at PTL. However, most of my requests of the Lord centered on the mechanics of moving and not enough on why and especially for whom. Even though I heard we were to go and minister to youth, making plans with the Lord to do just that unfortunately did not cross my mind.

We did some work with young people and their families while still in Connecticut but did not know specifically what we were to do in Aspen. However, Wayne had a sense of peace about moving as we continued to pray and seek the leading of the Lord.

It was our habit on Sundays to watch Oral Roberts on TV. On these programs, they never had pictures or anything to break up the preaching. However, on this particular morning, after receiving a firm word about moving to Aspen, we were watching the show, and without any explanation, all of a sudden on the screen was a series of mountain scenes—snow on the mountains, mountains in the springtime, and rivers with mountains in the background. It was a powerful confirmation to us. Again, there were no pictures of any kind during these programs previously or on any later shows. Therefore, based on His spoken words, the assurances we received during our prayer times, and the uncharacteristic pictures, we prepared to leave.

I desired to be water baptized before leaving PTL. I experienced salvation and the filling of the Holy Spirit but missed this step. Uncle Henry, the television announcer, agreed to make a special time at the pool for us, and he immersed me in water as a symbol of my desire to do all that is right before the Lord. I was in great expectation that something miraculous would happen. What I realized later is the miracle was I did not have any uncomfortable fears over lack of finances or about anything else anymore as we charted unknown waters again. I was totally at peace and had faith to go forward during this transition time.

We left joyfully, in faith, and with great anticipation, with our girls and the cat, motor-homing cross-country via typical tourist attractions.

After arriving in Aspen and driving down Main Street, we saw young people on both sides of the road and all around. It is a young persons' town because of the varied skiing venues and summer activities, like hiking, kayaking, and river rafting. Seeing all of this was another positive confirmation that we were to settle here and work with youth.

We parked in a quiet state campground when we first reached the area. However, we quickly used up the maximum stay of five days. It was almost September and time for the girls to begin school. We did not have a suitable place to stay the night before their first day.

There was one more campground farther up toward Independence Pass. We hadn't been in this mountainous area before because we questioned if our heavy rig would tolerate the trip. However, we had no choice, believing we needed to live in the Aspen vicinity when school started.

Starting to climb to the pass made it abundantly clear the motorhome was excessively large for this road. With rising mountains on the driver's side and a sheer drop-off on mine, the motorhome was struggling with the grades and threatening to choke out. But there was no way to turn back. I was white knuckled all the way up. I prayed continuously on that mountain. A small campground finally appeared at an elevation of about ten thousand feet. We just backed in as the engine heat gauge hit its maximum.

The next morning's downhill drive concerned me greatly. "What about the brakes?"

We had water and electricity on board, but the campground did not have either. In the afternoon, a young man came by who was biking the pass.

He was on his way to Aspen to be part of the ski scene but was terrified with the traffic going around him; it was treacherous. He came to the campground looking for water and rest.

We invited him in, provided water and homemade breakfast cake just as it started sleeting. As we got to talking, we found it easy to share the Lord with him. We could tell he was interested and open to the real God. He decided to pray the prayer of salvation with us and before he left committed his life to the Lord.

We gave him the only Bible we had to give, which weighed quite a bit. I was a little concerned about that

58

extra weight on his bike, but he received it gladly. We believed this was one more confirmation we were to be there for younger people.

The Lord often mentioned meeting the needs of His people to me in my prayer times, but the reality of doing anything about it seemed so far off. He provided protection over us and met our needs during these early few weeks, but I had not asked Him the basics like, "What do we do here? How do we serve? Whose needs can we meet and how?" He showed His patience and forgiveness of me for all the times I was with Him and simply did not ask.

Now what were the answers to those questions? And would I ever ask?

8. Aspen the First Time

Driving a big rig into Aspen requires negotiating a narrow busy two-lane highway nestled among wooded ridges and barren cliffs. Mountain peaks are fully in view nearby. The road often drops off, leading precipitously down to the Roaring Fork River. The intriguing trip ends with two ninety-degree corners, then directly into the little resort town. Jubilantly driving down Main Street, we saw sidewalks populated with young people at leisure and colorful Victorian homes dotting the surrounding area.

It was exciting to be in Aspen, but immediately we hit a significant challenge: accommodations for the motorhome. The town is set up primarily to lodge short-term vacationers. After staying those first days in state campgrounds, we discovered that all of these facilities closed down in winter. Now where? There was no commercial campground in the immediate area, and even the KOA, farther down the valley, was set up for only short-term use. I was undeterred, knowing something would work out; otherwise, why would the Lord send us here?

We approached the existing mobile home parks. One had no room for a motorhome; they simply had no desire to help us in any way. The other, down along some railroad tracks, let us stay for two weeks behind their laundry on a temporary basis. Wayne was growing uneasy with the lack of even a semi-permanent place to stay. We asked the Lord to show us an answer.

Driving up and down the valley highway to dump waste and buy propane, we spotted one more mobile home

61

park off in the distance and across the river. We hastily drove to it and observed one empty site. When we tried to reason with the owners, a firm no was spoken from behind their partially closed door. The wife continued their negative response, stating, "The park is for long-term mobile homes only." Long-term was their dominant requirement. Running out of time to find housing, I phoned at least twice insisting we wanted to stay permanently. Finally, she reluctantly agreed to talk with us but said, "I might have already rented it."

After coming into our rig to check it out and visiting with our family, the wife finally agreed to let us have this last site. Smiling ear to ear, I felt relief and gratitude that the Lord answered our prayers by opening our eyes to see this one last park. I praise God for the victory!

After settling housing, our hopes were high, but income was zero and our limited funds were rapidly dwindling. I continually looked for jobs, but since I hadn't worked the prior year, opportunities seemed slim. The last job I held was in Connecticut as an electronics buyer for a small manufacturing company. The only abilities I developed as a buyer that could be useful in a resort area job were my skills with phone work. When I read a classified ad, "Reservationist Wanted," I was convinced in my heart this was my job. With letters of recommendation in hand, I pursued it with all confidence and hope in the Lord. I had that certain assurance of faith the position would soon be mine even though many had applied. A week and a half later, the Snowmass Resort Association hired me. I rejoiced in the Lord and thanked Him for this provision.

Up to this time, I drove the motorhome up and down the valley to drop the girls off at school and Bette at the bus stop into Snowmass while I walked the streets of Aspen looking for work. After a month or so, I was still looking for a job.

I developed a deep friendship with David, an acquaintance at church who had a solid commitment to the Lord. He told me about a job where he was working, painting house interiors and some wallpaper hanging. He offered it to me, and I accepted gratefully because we were down to $35.

The deal we made is that I would gladly take the job if I could be paid daily in the beginning. David quickly phoned the owner of the company to explain the arrangement. The boss agreed to it, and I began work the next day. We received this moment with joy as all things fell into place, orchestrated by God and just in time. This type of small miracle solution occurred many times over, but this particular one made staying in Aspen within our grasp.

When work started, it became clear I was completely over my head. While doing trim work in an expensive home, I had trouble painting a window frame behind the sash lock. It seemed to take forever, and the boss came to me shortly after. He did not say he was upset with my slowness or desire for perfection but asked if I knew how to hang wallpaper. This trade requires careful attention to detail and carries a rather strict set of procedures. The job was actually a better fit for me, more in line with my tendencies. I did not know how but said, "I'm a fast study. Just show me the basics and I'll be able to do it." I had no background at all to be able to say that, but once again, the words just came out of my mouth, obviously formed by the Lord before I even realized they were in my mind. It showed the nearness of God and His favor. The Lord surrounded me with His peace and patiently walked me through handling the tools and the details of the trade. It quickly seemed like I had done this for years, and He made it possible for me to learn easily and turn into a valuable paperhanger.

David was aware that driving the motorhome over snow-covered roads would not work as permanent transportation in the Aspen area. Several months earlier, as we were moving toward Aspen, the Lord told me clearly the first thing we needed to do was buy a car. Unfortunately, fear and disobedience came upon me; I did not see how to do it financially, so I let it drop. Even later, the Lord told me again and gave me details of how to do it, but out of fear, I let it pass that time too. God is amazingly patient!

Then, one day at work, David told me a story about his older Lincoln car. He laughed and shared that in his younger days, he took off the fenders and drove it into the mountains just for fun as if it was a four-wheel drive vehicle. They did not have a plan for it, but it ran fine and he had put all the pieces back together.

David and Marlene decided to give us that Lincoln. We were shocked, amazed, and full of thanksgiving for the two of them and the Lord. They simply gave it to us, beautifully out of love, and that became our first easy transportation up and down the valley. The Lincoln was a blessing to have, but after a while, the transmission started to fail. The repairs were going to cost a minimum of eight hundred dollars, probably much more.

After discussing options with David, he finally said, "Well it's your car now; do whatever you think best." I did some research on new and used cars in *Consumer Reports* at the library and called around to several dealers. I found one who said, "We can work something out." I believed his offer and felt nudged by the Lord to take all four of us into Denver that weekend. It was Saturday.

We intended to see if we could make a deal on a four-wheel drive Subaru using the motorhome as collateral. Full of faith and trust in the Lord, we went expecting success.

We were close to Denver, just climbing the last upgrade, when suddenly the transmission made a heart-stopping explosive "bang," a grinding noise, and the car started to slow down. This last steep portion of the highway almost shattered our plans. However, with our focus fixed on the Lord and with prayer, the Lincoln made it all the way up. We limped noisily into the dealership, parking way in the back hoping they would not hear us.

Going inside we found the salesman I talked to on the phone who worked hard to find a car that would meet our needs. He did. However, when it came time to work with the finance man, he informed us we could not use the motorhome as collateral to finance another vehicle. Now all we had to give them was this failing Lincoln.

We held our breath and continued to pray as the salesman took the keys and drove it around the lot to check it out. We did not even consider what would happen if it failed completely. Faith filled the air.

They offered us one hundred dollars for the car. Being late on Saturday, the finance person did as well as possible to check our credit. He insisted we put some cash down, but we didn't have anything more than food and gas money in our checkbook. Bette, the girls, and I joked among ourselves that if they did not sell us a car, we would actually be living in Denver. We were not afraid, just amused and full of godly assurance all would be well.

It took hours while the salesman continued going back and forth between the finance office and us, but we stood strong in the confidence that the Lord told us to drive over this weekend.

The miracle God moment occurred after intense prayer, when they finally accepted the Lincoln as full down payment. It was nightfall driving away celebrating and rejoicing in recognition of what the Lord had just done.

We were in our brand new, fully accessorized, red, four-door, four-wheel drive Subaru. Even the bright red and orange glowing dashboard awed us. That Saturday night we had a wonderful drive home, back over the mountains in a light powdery snowfall.

Sunday we joyfully shared this glorious moment with our church friends. Within just a few days, the heavy mountain snows started, beautiful but sometimes daunting. Hearing the solid, smooth *thump* when it dropped into four-wheel drive was one more comforting proof of the power of God.

A week later, the salesman called, saying, "The title is in the name of another couple in Aspen, not you." I explained we simply forgot to transfer it, but I would send the title to him. I realized that getting a new car with no down payment or even ownership of the trade-in is impossible in the natural. It seems as though the Lord impressed a "yes" on the finance person's mind and a forgetfulness about the title on the salesman's mind. Praise God!

We now had housing, transportation, and jobs and planned to settle into a comfortable routine. However, several weeks later we were chatting comfortably while driving home and were greeted by a glaring red tag hanging on the motorhome door. I exclaimed, "Now what?" It said the county was citing us for being in noncompliance and that we had to move within seven days.

We prayed and asked the Lord to show us a way through the problem. I said to Wayne, "Why don't you call and see what is going on?" He called the Pitkin County Zoning department and talked to the person in charge, who checked the citation and was adamant that we simply could not stay.

Then I experienced another one of the special situations where God speaks words through me before I form the thoughts in my mind. Rather than simply accepting the difficulty, the Lord asked through me, "What is the county statute that applies to this red tag?" He dismissively said that he did not care what we did but wanted us to know we had to leave. In a huff of frustration, he said it was too late in the day for this stuff and refused to look up the actual regulation.

Again, Wayne respectfully asked that he read off the statute just as written. Finally, the zoning official relented, looked up the ordinance, and read it to Wayne word for word.

First, we must be at least thirty-two feet long. I said firmly, "We are, exactly!" Permanently connected was what it emphasized next.

It was not until Wayne understood this that I saw a glimmer of hope on his face. The Bible talks about speaking to authorities. Although the following Scripture context refers to the end times, it was also applicable in this situation.

> *But make up your mind not to worry beforehand how you will defend yourselves. For I will give you words and wisdom that none of your adversaries will be able to resist or contradict. (Luke 21:14–15)*

I felt comforted with this God moment, when the Lord gave Wayne the right words and was about to give him a possible solution.

At this point, I needed to figure out a way to meet the requirements. All we had so far was water connected temporarily by a hose and our sewer needs met by dumping waste at the KOA facility. Besides, with winter coming on, I did not know how to keep the pipes from freezing even if I did connect them properly.

We soon learned that Aspen winters are much more severe than we expected. We needed to find a permanent solution because our rig would not tolerate these conditions out in the open.

Now I needed to work out a way to make the connections. I am mechanically inclined but needed confidence and assurance from God before I was comfortable attempting this work. The Lord orchestrated it so simply that to connect the rig up to the sewer opening near the site was no more difficult than picking up some lengths of pipe and a few fittings and learning how to make the necessary glue joints. The fittings came from two unrelated suppliers, but they fit together perfectly. To connect the water in an acceptable manner simply required a particular type of heat tape that worked on a garden hose; it only heated up when exposed to freezing temperatures. I also wrapped the hose in thick insulation and duct tape that made it appear permanently attached.

Both systems worked perfectly. After doing this work, we asked the county inspector to come and check out the installation. He did. The red tag was removed.

When winter's cold and snows were imminent, we put plastic-wrapped plywood around the perimeter of the rig. As a result, the motorhome felt warm and cozy even though temperatures dropped well below zero. These efforts firmly connected us to the ground. The only things visible that told people we were not a mobile home were the headlights and windshield. This then became our first Aspen housing. A sense of belonging flooded over me.

One more event showing how the Lord works is when I refilled the propane tanks before they ran out, it meant I had to approximate their percentage of use. One day while waiting at the RV store, I saw a gadget that automatically switched the flow of propane from an empty tank to a second full one. As I briefly scanned over the fully stocked store, I almost passed over this mechanism. However, the Lord drew my attention to the inexpensive device. After looking over the claims, I bought and quickly installed it. This simple little God-given improvement meant we would have consistent heat and hot water. In addition, when it switched over, it was easy and convenient to see when a tank needed refilling.

The challenge of the red tag event actually strengthened our ability to survive comfortably in this new environment. God amazed me constantly with His faithfulness to see things through. It certainly increased our faith as He confirmed His intimate involvement with us.

9. Test the Spirits or Be Led Astray

One event that showed me how easily I fell into a spiritual battle was when I saw a vision-like daydream while driving home after work. It was of a dirt road on the side of a mountain with a house up above on a plateau looking out over a valley. The Lord mentioned in prayer several times that we needed a house. I believed the Lord was showing me the home we were to have in Aspen.

So month after month, every weekend, we traipsed into the mountains around Aspen. We went on foot, car, snowmobile, a rented helicopter, and the pastor's small airplane searching for this house. As we drove up and down the valley and looked up on both sides into the mountains, I could imagine the areas where the house might be. However, we stopped looking when it became clear we blanketed the entire area in our search and found nothing.

Very discouraged, I finally spent a great deal of time in prayer with the Lord. I also resumed journaling. I essentially stopped doing both while we were looking for this nonexistent house. When I asked God about all of this and asked if this vision was of Him, He said decisively:

> No, son. I spoke to you at Mountain Valley [at work] to go and find your house. The words that I spoke to you are true and can be trusted: "You are to work and play and learn in Aspen. You may live anywhere." You have heard many words, some of Me and some not. I have told you

many times to test every word that you hear. And how do you test these words? By repeatedly coming to Me in faith and hearing from Me. But you have not done this. Did you not realize that everything you have based your search on has been received in turmoil, confusion, frustration, and rebellion?

And how much time have you spent before Me? Son, if you will continue to stand before Me and spend time with Me—much time—you will soon be at peace again, and your family will start to flourish again. And your relationship with Bette will become soft, and the demonic influence will be gone.

I called you to find your house. The Devil knew that also. But because you did not come to Me but chose rather to spend much time "thinking," you were prey to be diverted off this way and that.

You spent hours and hours and hours at My feet concerning the motorhome. Do you remember the cross and candle and carpet in Connecticut? You spent hours with me. Look in the books [journals] and you will see. I have better things for you than a tiny house far away from life, cold, and full of problems! I have called you *to* My people, not to be isolated from them.

I swallowed hard and felt ashamed. I wasted much time, effort and money following a flawed image.

Dear friends, do not believe every spirit, but test the spirits to see whether they are from God. (1 John 4:1a)

We all believed it was real, but just believing in something without being close to God Himself is not what faith is all about. This correction was difficult but necessary for us to learn.

No discipline seems pleasant at the time, but painful. Later on, however, it produces a harvest of righteousness and peace for those who have been trained by it. (Hebrews 12:11)

We did see some of the Rocky Mountains around Aspen quite thoroughly. We walked backcountry roads, hiked through hip-deep snow, realizing the value of snowshoes we did not have, and drove on unpaved roads we never would have considered under normal circumstances. One Trail ended at an elevation of 12,800 feet. We saw some of the mining history, beautiful columbine, and alpine wildflowers in an array purple, blue, and pink. However, sadly, we missed God!

.

10. Build a Product

Praying ardently in faith, I asked the Lord, "What is really going on here? Bette is working full time, but I can only find on-again, off-again work as a tradesman. I need regular, substantial income. Lord, what can I do in Aspen? What should I look for? Do I want service work like a waiter job in a year-round restaurant? Or do You have something in mind for me to do?" Quite by surprise, the Lord said,

> Stop asking questions, stop talking,
> and listen intently to Me.

The voice of God was certain and assured but also full of life, as though something big was about to happen. His all-encompassing presence and words filled my entire being.

All of a sudden, a concept about a new product, never seen before, flooded my mind. He showed me in my mind's eye an overview of how the product would look. He explained many details about what it did but not how. That was for me to discover. It was fantastic when I got a glimpse of the answer. The flow of ideas continued over several days. I was fascinated and fully absorbed in this event. How could I not be?

After letting this all sink in, I accepted the potential solution with open arms. It felt good. I was totally optimistic, confident, and looking forward to being creative and flowing with Him.

God had spoken. His voice and manners were recognizable: authoritative but calm, firm yet gentle and kind. After hearing His words and intuitively envisioning the product, I also received understanding of its broad applications. The Lord made it clear that producing and selling it was going to be the answer for our income.

As I sought the Lord in prayer, He continually said, "Meet the needs of My people." This was the work ahead of us. However, I thought this included meeting our basic needs before giving anything of substance to other people. I assumed this product was to be the means to accomplish both goals. However, the Lord was not talking purely about finances.

In an atmosphere of peace, my husband revealed the details of his time with the Lord. Reverential awe was all over Wayne. It was evident to me that he had a profound time with the Lord, and I was enthralled to hear about the experience. His enthusiasm was so strong and contagious that after soaking it all in, I found myself in full support of this new endeavor.

I began by experimenting with the elements used in the product in the living room of the motorhome. The excitement of creativity filled our space. Spending most of my time discovering how this fragile concept worked required much learning, but as I spent quiet time with the Lord, asking specific questions, He always answered.

My heart was hopeful as we followed the Lord in this project. However, I knew my most valuable contribution was to keep producing income at my current job. Wayne continued working part-time jobs, but he worked on the product during his slack time. The highlight of my day was coming home at night and hearing about Wayne's progress.

It soon became clear that we needed some help to move this project ahead. We found an engineer and a cabinetmaker at church who assisted in building a model of the product.

In addition, we needed room to produce this prototype. We owned a screen house from camping trips back in Connecticut and continued carrying it with us in the motorhome. The Lord told Wayne to set up this screen-sided tent next to our rig and do it rather firmly, not temporarily, even though it was far from a permanent structure. It was a pleasant surprise as He guided us to create this construction area out of practically nothing.

All through the time we developed the product and built the first model, I stayed close to the Lord in my prayer times. It was an exciting time of communication and fellowship between the Lord and myself.

The goodness of God came through constantly. When He would tell me to do something on the product, I would do it and it would work. As I continued to ask Him, He showed me detail after detail in order to get through the various stages of development.

However, the Lord's directions were not paint by number but more like a thousand-piece picture puzzle with many parts to find and put into place through trial and error. And they were not like a smorgasbord where I could choose what I wanted to receive. My thoughts were often nowhere near His.

As a result, I did not understand everything simply by listening to Him. Although His words in prayer explained much, we still needed to engage our God-given talents with Him. We spent a solid year using our creative abilities, Bette's knowledge and skills as an electronics component buyer, and much of our limited funds to reveal the Lord's amazingly simple and elegant solution to a well-known problem in this field.

It was late fall and cold when the first model was completed. The God-given concepts and components came together perfectly, and the team actually produced a functioning product. We needed somewhere to set it up indoors, and the new pastors agreed to give it a place in their house.

We were full of joy! It was finished, right?

11. Investors

We needed much money to bridge the gap between the prototype and a market-ready, well-priced product. It functioned but was a long way from being finished; we needed funds now, but they were hard to come by. We were able to locate some investor capital from friends, but more needed to be continually flowing in. It did not. We worked by the seat of our pants.

We needed to do some expensive work but I told the Lord I did not see how we could do it with our current income. I said, "We simply don't have the money." I should have gone to the Lord in deep prayer, just being close to the Father, and ask, "How do I get this paid for?" Then, I should have said, "Yes, I will do it; show me how." I know the Lord would have honored that prayer, but I did not ask.

Thinking a breakthrough was close; I quit my job to join the team and became the parts buyer. With much effort and due diligence, we devoted nine months of working full time to produce the first prototype and get the company formed. We made bootstrap efforts to keep going, even putting some additional funds into the company by taking out a bank loan against the motorhome.

Time after time, the Lord gave me the requirement to find investors. He requires that I obey quickly and completely. I found myself resisting because I did not know how to do this on my own. The Lord told me the place where I could fail was if I relied on my own thoughts of what to do rather than depending fully on Him.

Trust in the Lord with all your heart and lean not on your own understanding; in all your ways acknowledge him, and He will make your paths straight. Do not be wise in your own eyes; fear the Lord and shun evil. (Proverbs 3:5–7)

Mechanical things are clear to me, but I lack financing and marketing skills; they are foreign to me. I simply have no previous experiences to draw from. I could not give faith-filled responses to the Lord's instructions as I did while creating the product itself. I didn't even know enough to ask the Lord good questions about what to do next. This was a time of discouragement. Regardless, the Lord was merciful; often at the end of my prayer times, the Lord would say, "Be at peace, son. I love you." That comforted me and settled me down somewhat during the times of depression and confusion that soon would become constant.

At one point, while complaining and praying about the delay in not finding investors, the Lord said these words, which I wrote down in my prayer journal:

> [Delays] come from waiting rather than receiving. When you receive a gift from someone, you must take it from his or her hands. If you simply sit back and look at the person, the gift will be delayed, if given at all. When you go to an orchard, there is a delay until an apple drops. You can eat that way, but the fruit is not the best and there are delays.

You literally demanded [took and received] the knowledge of how to build the product and how to build the company. But you waited for money. You didn't reach out and take the money. Get every magazine and paper that has to do with money. Walk into the orchard and start to look around. Don't wait for "drops." But look for just the right apple. Then climb up and take it [receive]. There are Christians in the finance world too. Immerse yourself in the world of money, then come back and get My wisdom.

How do you receive fish? You get hooks in their mouths and *pull* them to you! And how about wheat? You *pull* it out of the ground and *beat* it in order to receive what I have provided! If you wait, you will find delay. If you take, you will receive.

I knew that good advice was missing on where and how to find investors.

Plans fail for lack of counsel, but with many advisors they succeed. (Proverbs 15:22)

Asking our accounting firm for leads to investors and even seeking out the Small Business Administration's state incubator for funds led us nowhere. My inexperience blinded me from seeing additional resources, and at the same time Satan placed negative thoughts in my mind such

81

as, *You are not good enough to do this! You do not know what you are doing! You are going to fail!* I did not know what else to immerse myself into; the magazines and articles seemed too general to meet our needs. A victory seemed so distant, even with the Lord urging us on.

Fear over the income issue overcame me. I let my Bible reading lapse into inactivity. I forgot how to live with Him by listening, obeying, and then going back to Him. However, if I continued to seek the Lord, He would have provided answers, not only as to what was needed and when but also how to do it.

Then, something alarming happened. A deeper than normal depression took hold of Wayne's emotions. He became overwhelmed. At this time we did not understand he was dealing with an undiagnosed flare-up of bipolar depression. This severe disorder stopped him from seeking the Lord, causing fear to run unchecked, and undermined the faith we so desperately needed.

If we stayed in absolute trust, in faith, and in prayer, we would have remained intimately connected to the Lord in everything we were doing. We did not.

I did not know how to deal with it. We dropped very low on money and hope. I felt ashamed asking our landlord if half the site rent would be good enough until I could raise more money. She allowed it, but I felt frightened and lost. Finding only temporary work helping a friend to do professional housekeeping, I discovered I was too inexperienced for that job.

One afternoon, coming home frustrated and tired, I met closed blinds with Wayne still in bed. My earthly leader was down for the count. He was obviously overwhelmed with depression; I lost hope as well, and we both became ineffective in prayer. What do I do now?

12. Defeat and Retreat

I made efforts to find work again, but the local seasonal jobs were no longer available and now we had a mortgage on the motorhome to pay. Waves of discouragement hit me when my search was not successful. I grieved giving up my good-paying job in Snowmass. This and the deep depression that came over Wayne made it seem as though all the gates of hell were against us. It seemed sufficient income was not attainable.

At that time we did not know to seek medical help for Wayne; we only saw the results of this undiagnosed illness. We dealt with the severe up-and-down mood swings throughout our entire married life. Now these looming circumstances seemed insurmountable. We arrived at a point of believing our only option was to retreat, pay off all the bills that were now overdue, and regroup.

After all of the incredible victories at the beginning—selling our house miraculously, seeing the Lord provide a marvelous motorhome, and having a blessed and happy time at PTL—we were finally pressured to leave Aspen due to our inexperience in handling the two crosses in our life: money and depression. Even though we were not in God's perfect will, He permissively accepted our decision to go back to Connecticut. We saw this as a necessary step, but to us it seemed like defeat.

The Lord still gave us mercy, comfort, and love in spite of our inability to finish what was set before us. We wanted to stay in Aspen because the Lord placed us there. We had some success in the church (we did run a youth group) and success with the product (it does still exist). Nevertheless, not only was the lack of money a defeat, but there was also a spiritual battle going on against us staying and succeeding. Leaving seemed to be the only way out of the struggle. The girls stayed behind to finish their school year by living at the pastor's house and caring for their children. Our plan left me feeling at a loss; I knew we couldn't stay, but I did not want to leave the girls.

February, our planned departure time, was in the midst of an unusual thaw. Because of it, the previously frozen motorhome skirt and bottom of the screen house defrosted just enough to remove. In addition, the engine started right up with just an oil change after not running for three and a half years. The battery was not even depleted! We were grateful to leave the site clean enough that they returned the full security deposit. These positive events surrounding leaving were all God moments to us.

Divorcing ourselves from the apparent defeat in Aspen, we looked to the Lord for comfort and refreshment. He successfully led us out on bare pavement through the mountains in winter without any snow or even icy roads.

Although my soul was in depression, my spirit was at peace. The Lord led me, by strong impressions, to a gorgeous out-of-the-way site in a state park near Phoenix, Arizona. We stayed a couple of nights soaking up the refreshing springtime.

Families of quail walked around freely, and the eerie sounds of coyotes echoed in the nearby hills. As we continued driving, we went through southern Texas, seeing brilliant red and purple sunsets that spectacularly filled the whole sky. The Lord comforted and blessed us during the entire trip and in all the quiet, nearly empty campgrounds. His presence provided a shield of peace all around us; we welcomed this reprieve from the pressures left behind.

On the way back to Connecticut, I felt a release from the barrage of thoughts that my personal inabilities were the sole source of our problems in Aspen. We were not aware of the cause of the deep depression I was suffering. We parked at my parents' house again when we arrived. Where to live permanently occasionally crossed our minds, but we did not intend to go back to Aspen.

I applied for a job with my old employer. The Lord obviously prepared the way for me because when I interviewed with my former boss, she said, "We were just talking about you the other day." I was comforted and encouraged with her response; my faith rose up again. She phoned a few days later and rehired me. Favor was also on Wayne as he was able to get a full-time job quite readily.

As part of our retreat, we reluctantly decided to sell the motorhome to Bette's parents. Although it was necessary to relieve our debts, I was saddened that the season of that beautiful rig ended. Nevertheless, since selling the motorhome worked and the jobs came easily, we settled into a comfortable routine.

When we talked with the girls after they flew back to Connecticut, we found they accepted that leaving Aspen was necessary but they were also disappointed. They were able to visit and spend a day at the local school but the general characteristics of the education system and the large class sizes distressed them. As a result, both of our daughters had a strong desire to finish their junior and senior years in Aspen. They found great success in its school programs by taking advanced classes and being very strong on the debate team.

We needed to make a decision very soon about whether to go back or stay since fall was rapidly approaching. We both prayed a great deal, went for long walks, and discussed what we should do. Finally, Wayne said, "I think the Lord is telling me we have to go back." I agreed.

We were comfortable with returning even if the main reason was to honor our daughters for their sacrifices and hard work. So determined to fight the battles of jobs and housing one more time, being out of debt again, and having encouragement from the Lord, we found ourselves driving west. Still, the defeats in Aspen that were painfully recent raised unavoidable concerns. What would we find this time?

13. Aspen the Second Time

The cross-country trip west passed uneventfully, and I found my mind calm and peaceful, knowing a homecoming back to the familiar part of Colorado was coming soon. My commitment to the mountains and even to Grand Junction on the west and Denver to the east was very real. I emotionally accepted Colorado as home. Driving in the waning light of evening, I anticipated our arrival in Aspen the next day.

Shifting into a lower gear as we neared a Denver exit, the clutch pedal suddenly fell lifelessly onto the floor. The clutch had failed. Being in second gear, the car limped down the exit and without stopping wound its way onto the adjacent road. Bette quickly spotted the parking lot of a hotel; I pulled into a space and immediately came to a distressingly abrupt stop. It was not going to move again without repairs.

I was grateful and thanked the Lord we were just turning onto an exit rather than in the middle of the highway. My hands were shaking as I fumbled through my discount hotel coupon book and found a listed inn right in front of us. Thank You, Lord. After gratefully checking into a beautiful and inexpensive one-bedroom suite, Theresa helped me carry in our heavily laden suitcases, unpack, and get us set up for the night.

Wendy and I went outside to look at our immobilized car.

I was praying continually for wisdom for Wayne and trusting the Lord for a solution but I was exhausted and just wanted the night to end. What did my husband and daughter expect to find in the dark, out in the open, in the outskirts of Denver?

Half-expecting to find a pool of oil under the car or a smoldering hiss of smoke or steam from an obvious crack in the engine, I cautiously opened the hood and panned the flashlight onto the motor. Nothing seemed obvious.

I wondered what a problem deep down in the car would do to our limited funds

And how could we travel on to Aspen? I was not as confident as usual. What parts failed, and where were they? Wendy moved the pedal, but nothing moved under the hood. What do I do now, Lord?

Moving the pedal back and forth created only the smallest rubbing sound near the engine. Tracing the tiny noise to a cable and following it revealed it traveled between the pedal and a lever on the engine. However, nothing moved, so could the problem be a break in that cable?

I looked up to the Lord and felt an assurance this was the problem, and quite naturally, the Lord provided an auto parts store within easy walking distance the next morning. The clutch worked perfectly after I installed a new cable. The Lord continued to show us that He could solve potentially costly problems like this one with relatively simple and inexpensive fixes.

Finally, I could breathe again! This crisis was over. Now with the car repaired, we were able to continue on the following day. I felt great relief as I rested in the assurance that the Lord was with us.

Arriving back in the Aspen area, we stayed in a small resort hotel, again in the coupon book. A search of the surrounding area for an apartment to rent—actually

anything to rent—was unsuccessful. Still trusting in the Lord, I had a surprising chat with the night auditor that led to a property in town that gave her friend an excellent rate. Could this be an answer? Hope rose up in my heart.

Under a brilliant blue sky, the sunny decks on the Concept 600 apartment building presented a bright prospect. However, the Realtor in charge said nothing was available to rent. One was for sale, and the owner already moved out. It had been on the market for a long time, and she wondered if the owner might talk to us about renting. We would have to talk with him directly, but she offered to call him and ask if he would be interested. He was. Shortly after we met with him, the familiar peace of God flooded over me with a confidence this would work out. The apartment was more than acceptable, and we made the deal, with the provision that when it sold, we would have thirty days to move out. Even so, I sensed a quiet peace that afternoon as we drove into the covered parking and rode the elevator.

Gratitude filled my heart with God's amazing provision of housing. This beautifully furnished top-floor location had lots of sunlight. Since it faced Aspen Mountain, we could see all the skiing activity, including the New Year's torchlight descent. Being on Main Street and close to everything, it was nearly perfect. I was especially thankful to the Lord for this blessing because of the many little touches and details. Several gorgeous, large plants filled the living room, a mirrored wall flanked the dining area. Perfect bedroom layouts and a full modern kitchen completed this gift from God. I praise the Lord for this place since living quarters like this were particularly rare, especially in our price range.

However, what about money now that we solved the housing question?

It was another God moment when I quickly found full-time work at Colorado Central Reservations.

The manager let me know shortly after I arrived that she was fighting a life-threatening cancer. We became close friends, and I had the privilege to lead her to the Lord. Months later when I heard she died, it helped to know she was in heaven.

I realized another blessing when the owner moved the office to a downtown professional building and into a corner office that had many windows. The Lord gave me another significant moment with Him when the boss promoted me to the job of managing that company. The Lord's favor caused the firm to flourish.

I spent my time working small seasonal jobs until Bette's boss mentioned a property maintenance job opening. I received this lead as from the Lord and applied quickly, and Aspen Group, Inc. offered it to me immediately. It started out as a relatively simple fix-it job at one small lodge. The company grew rapidly in the property management business, and this position soon developed into a supervisory one over two hotels and two bed and breakfast inns. Not only was it busy during day-to-day activities in season, but a preventative maintenance program made the work full time. Eventually this job covered a very large number of rooms, all four of the mechanical facilities, two pools, and four spa tubs.

This excellent position gave us the financial stability I knew we needed. I was grateful for what I saw as two reliable incomes and being able to live in a beautiful apartment. It was pleasant to relax into a comfortable routine.

But then, the apartment sold!

We were in the housing battle again, having just thirty days to find a solution. Since the one flaw with the apartment was a great deal of noise, finding a new apartment felt undesirable. This problem did not cause me great consternation. I found myself strangely at peace. Because the Lord showed himself abundantly strong in providing housing up until now, why wouldn't He continue?

Our heart's desire was for a house, believing God would open up something good. The Bible encouraged us:

> *Do not be anxious about anything, but in everything, by prayer and petition, with thanksgiving, present your requests to God. And the peace of God, which transcends all understanding, will guard your hearts and your minds in Christ Jesus. (Philippians 4:6–7)*

We prayed wholeheartedly for this impossible dream.

My practical hope took form while driving through a part of town having numerous single-family homes. Imagining living in a house was easy for me; one had cut-glass windows sparkling in the streetlights, and many were beautifully painted in typical Victorian fashion. Any home was way beyond our reach at that time, but I fully joined my family in believing for a yet-unseen house.

Starting our search in the classified ads, we experienced a God moment event when that week's newspaper included a house rental in this prestigious west end of town. The owners were out-of-state teachers, and they rented it out during the winter season. The price was fantastic, and it would be a full house right in Aspen.

The only problem was that they retuned at Christmas break, and we would need to find other housing for those two weeks. Believing the Lord would handle this problem easily, even though it would be at the height of winter rental season, we were excited with this prospect. However, they said many people answered the ad, and they wanted to give all the respondents a fair chance. Several anxious days passed as we waited to hear their decision. Finally, the phone rang. Wayne answered. After a few moments of conversation, he turned to me and exclaimed, "We got it!"

Thank You, Lord! We were thrilled! The girls had plenty of room to entertain their friends, and it was a blessing for all of us to be able to live in a house again during the winter.

However, looming on the horizon was the move-out clause. I sought suggestions for Christmas lodging from my coworkers with no success. Searching intently for hotel space, in ever-widening circles, yielded no answers either. With our efforts being futile, we depended on the Lord to meet this need. Of course He did and in His characteristically surprising manner. As it neared time for the owners to come back, they phoned saying they changed their plans. The announcement was outstanding! They decided not to come out for Christmas. Talk about a God moment! We lived in that house undisturbed the entire winter season.

The Lord blessed our daughters, and because of His continual involvement in their lives, the twins finished Aspen High School with honors and scholarships and were valedictorian and salutatorian of their graduating class.

However, now that summer was arriving, this house opportunity closed. Where next?

After praying, I received an impression from the Lord to ask my employer if we could stay at one of his properties. He allowed us to stay in a small one-bedroom unit at the Hotel Aspen, in a wing undergoing construction. The cramped sleeping arrangements were difficult but they worked, and having this short-term housing available was another blessing.

As the off-season construction neared its end, the housekeepers needed to deep clean our quarters. It was also time for Theresa's college orientation. She chose Ithaca College in New York state for their impressive physical therapy program, so we all drove out to see the school. While the campus looked great, the only reasonable accommodations were hot dorm rooms with bunk beds. The heat and humidity were oppressive compared to the mountains back home.

Wayne and I did not have much time to talk since we were in separate men and women's dorms, but he told me later that he did pray fervently. I found my mind drifting into wondering what our next housing would be when we got back to Aspen?

Previously, while looking for rentals, a business contact invited us to see his house that was up for sale. It was not particularly expensive, but it was not for rent. After seeking God quietly in the empty dorm room, the thought came to me to call this owner and ask again if there wasn't some way we could rent.

However, when he was asked about this, he said, "No, I need a down payment to pay off my father, who fronted me the cash to buy it." Therefore, he could not just rent it out long term, and there was no way a second mortgage would work. The amount he needed was $10,000. It seemed like an impasse.

While praying about this and being in His presence, I realized we had exactly that amount on two unused credit cards. We could make the down payment.

After confirming this plan by laying it out before the Lord, I called him from the dorm payphone and said, "We will take it."

It was such a blessing that we were going to own a house and could move into it immediately upon returning home. It started out with a seven hundred–dollar payment for one month, long enough for us to do the mortgage paperwork. The Lord's intimate involvement provided a house on Lighthill Road in a small development. The community was mountainous, with views of the Old Snowmass Valley. We could see lights beaming from grooming vehicles on Snowmass ski runs at night and views of Sopris Mountain, an extinct volcano, by day. It had a great deal of sunlight, with three bedrooms and a large room where Wayne continued developing the product in his spare time. Actually owning our own home in the greater Aspen valley was miraculous and very settling. We were full of joy and gratitude to the Lord for all the events that made this possible.

14. Bipolar Illness

While enjoying the stability and comfort of the Lighthill house, I devoted myself wholeheartedly to my job but never stopped long enough to spend sufficient time with the Lord. I always performed my work in maintenance with a high degree of extremely goal-oriented perfectionism. My high self-esteem drove me to believe I could do anything. I saw this job as requiring a commitment to be available twenty-four hours a day, seven days a week, tied to the phone and a pager.

Mania made it possible for him to handle these duties at first, and it seemed like he had everything under control. His stellar performance did not seem alarming. However, the pressures of it soon brought on and worsened a now-familiar and typical depression. Wayne gradually fell victim to drinking and smoking, as he did before he met the Lord. As time went on, the job took a severe toll on his emotions.

Then a dangerous release of chlorine gas unexpectedly occurred in a small underground pool equipment room. The room was always wet, as it was directly under a hot tub. Access was via a low, tight crawlway over gravel to a ladder going down under the tub. The gas escaped when I opened a fresh container of dry tablets that somehow became wet. The chlorine cloud billowed up and filled the small room quickly. In a panic, I stumbled up the ladder, crawled through the narrow access way, and pushed the door open just before being overcome by the poisoned air.

This frightening event, a growing weariness from the relentless battle with my emotions, and wanting to retreat into the business of working on our product led me to resign my position. I grasped at an imaginary hope and convinced myself during this depression that we were very close to bringing this new product to market. We were not. I hadn't been at peace for some time nor spent enough time in prayer to have made this major decision. The scourge of depression had hit in force and was pulling support out from under us again.

Thankfully, the Lord, according to His nature, never left us.

> *The Lord himself goes before you*
> *and will be with you; he will never*
> *leave you nor forsake you. Do not*
> *be afraid; do not be discouraged.*
> *(Deuteronomy 31:8)*

After a while, the depression seemed to lift, and we believed the product project could start moving ahead again. Wayne built a new prototype that was successfully a show model. We drove back east to reveal it to a newly formed marketing team. At that point, we were back to finding investors again, receiving advice from the team in Massachusetts, and getting ready to make a practical product.

The new product built at the Lighthill house was much more complete and effective than the original prototype. However, all during this time I continued the wild up-and-down emotional cycles, going from disproportionately high energy and activity down to the depths of depression. The spiritual attacks magnified the negative thoughts of failure and hopelessness and heightened the wild mood swings. As a result, the success of the product seemed to be in jeopardy.

Many times I would hear Wayne quote the first half of the Proverb that says,

> *Hope deferred makes the heart sick,*

without the last half,

> *but a longing fulfilled is a tree of life. (Proverbs 13:12)*

I am convinced that quoting only part of that Scripture was an attack from Satan to discourage Wayne further. He was again at the point in depression where he lost hope.

Work had to be my focus through these times. It allowed me to do something productive by bringing in income until Wayne's attitude allowed him to see things in a bright light again. I assumed better times would follow in the same pattern as they had in the past. Ignorance allowed me to think this was the normal way to deal with life. Needing medical help never occurred to me. Before Wayne's diagnosis as bipolar, I did not know how to deal with the depression that would overwhelm him other than to provide income and emotional support. However, far beyond that, the need for God's faithfulness and protection was rapidly approaching.

Bette was at work, I was depressed and drinking at home. The thought came into my head that perhaps someone in mental health could help my depression. I phoned the county mental health group in Aspen, who gave me an immediate appointment. The doctor misread and overreacted to my angry frustration with my mental condition as a threat of suicide. Soon someone behind me said, "Get up and put your hands behind you." They put me into handcuffs, stuffed me into a police cruiser, and drove away. I was ushered into a solitary cell, where I sat stunned.

It shook me when I got a call at work from the Aspen jail. The chaplain said, "Your husband is being held to protect himself." The Lord had intervened. The chaplain asked me to come and meet with him. He understood mental illness and talked about getting Wayne help. He searched for a place where doctors could work on his depression. An inpatient psychiatric program was located. I was relieved someone with more knowledge than I was going to work with Wayne and that help might be available.

I believe the Lord put a positive thought into Wayne's head to try to get help. They released him into my care, saying, "Your husband is not being held for anything other than his own welfare."

Then I had to find our car. Where was it? The police revealed it was at the Aspen Mental Health Department. Soon I reclaimed both car and husband. I needed to find and solve whatever was causing these problems. I was hopeful.

The chaplain located and arranged Wayne's admittance to the psychiatric facility near Denver. We made hasty preparations, and I drove Wayne over the mountains the next day. Halfway back over the mountains in the dark, it started to snow and sleet. Although I was alone and should have been frightened since Wayne usually drove on wintry roads, I had a peace from the Lord that everything would be okay.

While in that setting, I was finally diagnosed properly as bipolar and put on a medication that many patients use. However, this particular medication was not effective enough on the depth of my specific disorder.

We followed up with the psychiatrist from that facility, who worked with Wayne for several months.

The talking helped alleviate some of the conflicts and confusion. This gave me some hope, but I was still very much in the grasp of this terrible illness. Bette and I talked a great deal over the long trips back and forth to Denver. She asked, "Can the product be revived, or is it dead?" I really did not know.

15. One More Time

The thief comes only to steal and kill and destroy. (John 10:10a)

Satan made repeated attempts on Wayne's life. The first one came when we lived on Lighthill Road. We owned the house, and things seemed to be going well.

I was under the care of a psychiatrist, who freely prescribed antidepressants one on top of another, supposedly to solve side effects. They provided only agitation and nervousness, and I knew intuitively they were not helping me. Bipolar remained, and I had another event.

Another heavy depressive attack aided by alcohol occurred. It was nightfall. Wayne prepared to take the car. I knew something was definitely wrong. I raced down the stairs behind him, attempting to reason with him all the way to the car. Panic filled me as we fought over the keys. Forcefully grabbing them from my hand, he recklessly and violently gunned the car and raced down the driveway.

Bipolar was raging, and my mind struggled with severely negative thoughts. I left with the intention of driving into a bridge abutment. I removed the seatbelt and imagined my head crashing through the windshield. I expected to die. Rapidly driving down long straight stretches of road, I projected how fast I would need to go.

However, I could not do it due to the presence and awesome power of the Holy Spirit. I became confused and blinded from seeing clearly how to accomplish my plan. I just sat in the car on the side of the road, distraught and discouraged.

As soon as he left, I cried out to the Lord, realizing the severity of what I was dealing with. The thought came to call the Kenneth Copeland ministry for prayer. I quickly called. A gentleman on the phone prayed with me and told me to get into the Word and stay in the Word. Finally, Wayne came back home.

At that time, by the grace of God, I started to read Psalms. I read them out loud so the roar of fear would not overtake me. I heard Wayne drive into the garage and come up the stairs. Then it was quiet. I thought the event was over and he was in bed. I kept on reading Psalms in a whisper so as not to disturb him. I had just read Psalm 91 when suddenly there was a loud, heavy thud in the bedroom. Rushing around the corner and into the room, I instantly knew he was in crisis. He was conscious but incoherent on the floor. Full of dread, I struggled to get him onto the bed. Thinking to check his meds, I ran to the bathroom and found the sink full of empty pill bottles. He took absolutely all of his medications. In addition, most of them were just refilled.

When I realized what he had done, a holy, righteous anger rose up in me. Filled with faith I went to the foot of the bed, pointed my finger at Wayne, and shouted, "You will not die! No disaster will come near our tent! And there will be no residual effect from those medications!" The Scripture reference that came out of my mouth was,

> *then no harm will befall you, no disaster will come near your tent. (Psalm 91:10)*

It was the Lord, His Word, and the prayers of the ministry that gave me the courage to believe.

I called the emergency number of his local psychiatrist, who instructed me to tell the ambulance driver to take him to the Glenwood Springs hospital, forty-five minutes away. We found out later this doctor had lost his privileges at the Aspen hospital. When the ambulance came and the EMTs realized what happened, they insisted the closest hospital was Aspen and there was no time to lose. One of the medications he took was to slow the heart, as well as bipolar issues, and is absorbed within a few seconds. He had taken a whole bottle of it. The ambulance took off.

The ER doctor said it did not look good. They were pumping out his stomach, but he had taken medications that would take his life very quickly. I waited most of the night at the hospital and heard about two other suicide attempts that were still in comas and a third one who died. The doctor came out and matter-of-factly explained that for the moment, Wayne was still alive, but he did not want me to get my hopes up. They told me to go home.

When I woke up the next morning in the hospital, I felt fine. The nurse in the room encouraged me, but I said, "There is no reason I should be alive. I should be dead, and I want to be."

She responded with, "No, you have much to live for." When I asked what happened she said, "You tried to commit suicide. When you got here, we pumped out your stomach. It was an amazing thing. You took many pills. They should have all dissolved by the time you got here. But they were all intact! They were all whole!" It took over a half an hour to get me to the hospital, but no pills had taken effect on me. The Lord actually kept them from dissolving!

When I arrived back at the hospital in the morning, I waited for a shift change before they finally allowed me to see him. I was relieved to find him alive and alert. I did not know all that happened overnight until Wayne relayed the God moment of the pills. I was overjoyed at what the Lord had done! Again, God's faithfulness brought us through a major crisis.

I was taken from the hospital that morning handcuffed to Jim (a deputy), who happened to be a praying member of our church, and flown to the state psychiatric hospital in Pueblo, Colorado. I spent two and a half months learning much about manic/depression and the dual diagnosis of a mental condition mixed with substance abuse. They gave me many medications, trying to find a combination that would work on me, but still with limited success. However, I was feeling better, and the drive home after my release was joyful.

All of these events seemed to settle down, and much time passed. This resolution gave me hope that he was now fine. I did not see any real hint of the horrible depression that plagued us for so long.

16. And Again

I was at my desk wrapping up the day, when my boss, with a very somber expression on his face, called me over to him. Walking toward the conference room, he motioned me to go in, saying, "You have a call waiting, and you'll need to take it in here."

A solitary phone sat ominously at the far end of a long table. I picked it up, and the conversation started with the caller introducing himself as being from the Aspen sheriff's office.

"Do you know where your husband is?"

"Yes, he's at home."

"Do you know he bought a gun in Glenwood Springs?"

"That's not possible. I have the car!"

"Evidently he rented a car."

He informed me a female deputy would meet me at the house shortly. Soon, the deputy arrived and asked, "Is your husband here? When was the last time you saw him?"

"He's not here now but was when I left for work this morning."

"Did you fight? Are you having marital difficulties?"

"No, not at all."

"Is he violent or abusive?"

"No."

"Do you know what he took with him? Go check the closet."

Shock overwhelmed me as I found his side completely empty! I was stunned. The deputy finished questioning me, closed her notepad, and left. I felt very alone, again.

Immediately, I cried out, "Oh Lord, help! Lord, I do not know where he is, but You do. Please protect Wayne and keep him safe, and help me understand."

Due to the power of bipolar depression, the pressure of failure to bring the product to market, and my inability to find a new job, I decided to really call it quits on life and simply go ballistic. So, after sending Bette off to work, I hurriedly packed up all my stuff, called a taxi, rented a convertible, withdrew two thousand dollars, bought a 358-magnum revolver, and took off for Las Vegas.

Once there, I tried to find a call girl before ending it all. A bellman told me, with a laugh, "They are not legally available for hire in Vegas but in abundance in Reno."

So, armed with much liquor and money, I drove on. When I was far out in the desert, I decided to try out the gun. I loaded it, and when nightfall was coming on, I fired several shots off to the side of the car. Realizing I really intended to kill myself, I drank very heavily, and not realizing why, I got out of the car and walked a long way down the side of the road. Many eighteen-wheelers were flying by.

I was hallucinating from the alcohol, insufficiently medicated bipolar, and negative satanic thoughts when I walked alongside the sand that dusky night and decided to throw myself in front of a truck. The desert looked surreal and undefined in the waning light, appearing to have no horizon at all. I wondered if I had died. I figured that if I were already in hell then the trucks would just pass through me. But if I were alive, then it would be over quickly. When I walked out into the road, an earsplitting blast from the truck horn startled me so much that I jumped out of the way. I couldn't do it and realized my demise would be by the gun. After walking so far, I lost all sense of direction and could not see the car. Stumbling around disoriented for quite some time, I finally found it and drove away, stupefied.

Waiting alone at home was devastating. I called the credit card company to get a glimpse of his location. Nothing new showed up. The sheriff's department was also trying to find Wayne, but many long hours went by with no word. My feelings of shock and disbelief consumed me. None of my thoughts made any sense.

When I arrived in Reno, I rented a motel room. I asked for a room far away from noise and received one at the end of a hallway on the top floor. I took all of my stuff up, planning to make this my last stand. I walked around the balcony with the gun and planned on where I would do it. Later I was scanning the yellow pages for an escort service that would send me a girl to make my last days fully sinful. I already knew that suicide was a sin, and I thought I would just pile them all together. These negative demonic ideations and the depression weighed heavily on me. Instead, without much thought, I decided to call my Denver psychiatrist and leave a message stating what I was about to do. This call was obviously God inspired because less than an hour later there came a loud banging on the door, and then a demand: "Open up! Police!"

After disarming me, they unceremoniously took me to the front desk to pay up and then on to the state mental hospital. The Lord's moment of awesome power and love were with me even in this time when I was not with Him. A brief stay ensued, and after determining I was not a serious risk to others, they placed me on an involuntary plane trip to Denver and into a low-security alcohol treatment facility called Sobriety House. They agreed to hold me for three months while attempting rehabilitation.

Wayne and I kept in touch by phone during those long months. Through these calls and two short Saturday visits, we were able to begin going down the long road of healing and creation of a new level of trust. I always believed in forgiveness and attributed most of our difficulties to the bipolar disorder. I knew that if I committed to forgive him in my heart, the Lord would help me complete the process. When I fully accepted forgiving him for the pain caused by this bipolar/demonic/alcoholic event, my love for Wayne once again bubbled up inside of me. Without the Lord working closely with me through this time, our relationship would not have survived.

When I saw her love, forgiveness, and genuine joy that I was alive, the desire to keep going rekindled in my spirit. Her authentic attitudes created a cone of security around me that just would not go away. I was able to forget my recent abandonment of her and started back into sobriety and more hope. However, I wondered, could the threat of depression be wiped away forever? I did not know. However, now we could relax with our newfound appreciation of each other, seeing the power of God at work, and simply enjoying life. Couldn't we?

17. The Legal Separation

Of course, I was still vulnerable because of the up-and-down pressures of bipolar and the normally attendant alcohol abuse. I found a job with a pool company that bipolar mania quickly developed into a sales division. However, because I had only limited sales skills, and when the mania fed excessively high self-confidence failed, it quickly died. I hit bipolar depression big time. Alcohol abuse resurfaced, and even though my original position was available, I refused it when I could no longer perform.

Losing job after job bewildered me. The threat of another bipolar suicide attempt loomed large. The seemingly impossible duty of paying off major debts weighed heavily on me. My mental state deteriorated into profound hopelessness.

I went through this season of pressure by grasping for relief. Money was very tight. We had put ourselves into a financial hole. I did not see a solution and wanted a new start. Not being able to try solving problems is a depressive symptom while being willing to rise and start over is a manic one. I was experiencing a mixed episode and was in a fight-or-flight state of mind. I decided to flee. Although I was properly diagnosed as a bipolar disorder victim, the medication prescribed was not nearly as effective on me as it needed to be. I really did not want to leave my wife again, but looking at life through the dark veil of depression led me to believe I had no way out. I told Bette, "I just need to get away for a while."

I responded, "What do you mean 'get away'? To where? For how long? Why is this necessary?" I was calm in my questioning and expected good answers from him. None came easily. He was acting burdened by the debt of college loans and bills from the product. He could not explain himself clearly. I was sympathetic to his despair but simply did not understand what he would gain by leaving. I fully expected him to change his mind.

He continued receiving his (wrong) meds from a clinic, but no psychiatrist was on his case. Things were charging ahead rapidly. I was unable to stop them partly because I needed to focus my time on keeping my job through all of this and due to Wayne's determined rebellion against my efforts to reason with him.

Wayne bought a cheap, heavily used, little old blue motorhome and worked his days repairing and rebuilding it as he prepared to launch out on his own. It took over two months for him to get it road worthy, and I kept thinking every day that he would come to his senses. He would excitedly invite me to see his latest improvements, but I was dealing with an imminent loss. How could I be happy for him? Why was this happening? However, he was fully determined to leave, so I reluctantly resigned myself to the fact I could not change his mind and he would not.

I sought a Christian counselor to help me wade through my jumbled emotions. She helped me cope with the day-to-day situations, but my pain was so overwhelming that I found no real relief. Continually, reality showed many details for me yet to work out. While we tried to solve the problems with his decision, we realized legal counsel was necessary. The first lawyer we talked to said divorce was the only way for me not to be responsible for Wayne's future debts. However, neither of us were at peace with this answer; Wayne said he would not accept a divorce, and neither would I. We found a second lawyer who said a little-used option would be a legal separation. This sounded better to us, but it still required that we divide all our assets as if going for a full divorce.

Therefore, I had to sell our house. It turned out that, as Wayne was almost ready to leave, the Lord provided a potential buyer who was very interested. Now it was a matter of working out the arrangements. Wayne in his manic exuberance told the buyer all of the appliances worked perfectly. They did not. He left me to arrange for the repair of several. I was overwhelmed with the volume of work I needed to do, along with keeping my job. I was used to Wayne taking the lead in major moves. I felt abandoned. I was sad and became more so as these predicaments kept coming up.

I decided to leave midweek late in the day. Looking pensively back toward the house, I slowly drove away in my motorhome. I half expected to see Bette waving good-bye to me. She was not. Although the prospect of a new start was exciting to me, leaving carried with it an ominous tone; I did not know if I ever wanted to come back or if it would even be possible.

I remember when he pulled out of the driveway, I was numb after all the turmoil. I planned in advance to have a quiet communion with the Lord when this finally happened with a sample-size bottle of wine and a matzo set aside just for this time. I knelt in prayer and said, "Okay, Lord, it's just You and me now." I recommitted my trust in Him.

After Wayne left, I did not know how to make it financially but shortly the Lord blessed me with a surprise. I was working for Aspen Classic Reservations, and for Christmas, the owner took all the employees to dinner at the posh Aspen Club restaurant situated at the base of Aspen Mountain. Even the mayor, who was the former owner of the company, joined us. The atmosphere was festive, and the dinner was great. Nevertheless, I was totally on my own, trusting that the Lord would provide for every need.

There were obvious secrets going on, but I had no knowledge of what was coming up. They kept it from me. Then the owner stood up and spoke, but it took me a moment to understand what he was saying. He announced my promotion to vice president and that I would manage the new office opening in Basalt! Every time the Lord lifted me up, it was a God-designed event. I give all the praise and honor for this moment to the Lord.

However, as the evening ended, I drove home alone, in the snow, to a dark house. I missed Wayne tremendously. He and I dated and had been the best of friends since we were seventeen. Now after being married for thirty years, he was gone. During this time of sadness, I continued to seek the Lord and came across this Scripture:

> Do not be afraid; you will not suffer shame. Do not fear disgrace; you will not be humiliated. You will forget the shame of your youth and remember no more the reproach of your widowhood. For your Maker is your husband-the Lord Almighty is his name-the Holy One of Israel is your Redeemer; He is called the God of all the earth. The Lord will call you back as if you were a wife deserted and distressed in spirit-a wife who married young, only to be rejected, says your God. (Isaiah 54:4–6)

I felt as if the Lord wrote this just for me. I memorized these Bible verses, and they became my foundational Scriptures. This separation took a big chunk *out of my very being. However, I invited the Lord into my situation, and He turned my sorrow into joy.*

> *To comfort all who mourn, and provide for those who grieve in Zion—to bestow on them a crown of beauty instead of ashes, the oil of gladness instead of mourning, and a garment of praise instead of a spirit of despair. They will be called oaks of righteousness, a planting of the Lord for the display of his splendor. (Isaiah 61:2b–3)*

I drove to the Outer Banks and then the inland areas of North Carolina. After pulling away from Bette, I spent my time getting involved with the disco scene. I was rebelling against anything that was good. I became infatuated with a club dancer and even tried to invite out a young female clerk at a drug store. I was drinking heavily, and flirting with sin was easy to do. The first year passed quickly.

I planned to move to Atlanta and fully follow the club lifestyle. I played around with cross-dressing and thought I might take up doing stage shows as a female impersonator laced with humor. Although I was enjoying myself, the Lord, by His interventions, slowly moved me away from it all.

During this time away, I had a gnawing sense that prayers were being said about me. The knowledge that Bette was praying, and that she was into church, made me aware that God had not fully abandoned me. When an acquaintance asked me to go to a traditional church while I was in North Carolina, I found myself praising with my hands raised even though I was in a staid, quiet setting. I was not as separated from Bette and the Lord as I thought.

The Lord mercifully shielded me from completing plans to commit to things that would have sent me deeply in the wrong direction. I was refused training by a talent agency because she said I had too good of a male voice, even disguised. My neighbor asked whether Atlanta or maybe Denver would give me more comfort. I did not know. I started rethinking life. Obvious flaws in my thinking showed up often.

During our separation, the Lord not only protected Wayne from getting involved with someone else, but He also protected me. A situation came up where someone asked me out on a date. I started to consider accepting, but the Lord stopped me and said sharply, "No!" In my mind and heart, it settled any further thoughts in this direction. After twelve months passed, many people, even those at church, accused me of not facing reality. They advised me to just divorce and move on. However, in reading my Bible these words stood out:

> *"'I hate divorce,' says the Lord God of Israel" (Malachi 2:16a).*

The living Word stopped me and kept my heart at peace.

18. Bette's Financial Moments

After Wayne left, the Lord was with me as I faced the bills. An accountant at church felt prompted by the Lord to ask me if there was anything he could do to help. The first thing that came to mind was a $5,000 computer package Wayne bought that was advertised as being an income-producing program, but I didn't know how to use it. When I called them and asked if I could return it, they flatly said no.

Wayne purchased it with one of our credit cards. At first, the accountant advised me to contact the card company to see if I could dispute the charge, but I found the sixty-day window to do this had just expired. When I reported this back to him the next Sunday, he said, "Let me see what I can do." He contacted the program company, including reaching all the way up to the president. He did all the phone work and followed up. He finally got them to agree that if I packed it up the way they delivered it; they would take it back and give me full credit.

When I explained I did not even know how to disassemble it, he helped me pack it up and even got it shipped. I was so grateful for his help, which made this such a God moment time for me. I remember at the next church meeting, the pastor asked if anyone had a praise report. I had the joy to be able to stand up and announce the Lord delivered me from a $5,000 debt that week. I was so awed by what the Lord had done.

Now I had to find a new home or pay taxes on the sale of the former one. By the time I figured up all the debt to pay off, it only left a little bit of money to put down on a new house. I located a mortgage person and found I could get an ARM-type loan that I could afford.

The next step was to look for houses. I was able to get a Realtor friend to help me find one. I started looking at the houses in my price range, but they were horrible. They were all run down and needed major repairs. I considered one nice-looking house in a new development, but I learned it had major building code violations, including the gas line. Clearly, that house would have been a money pit; buying it would have put me in deep financial trouble.

Finally, I saw everything available in my price range between Basalt and Glenwood Springs. Prices were high and inventory was low; nothing was even close to workable. I went home after going through this disheartening process, sat on the sofa, and in faith wrote out an impossible list of my desires and laid it before the Lord. I asked Him for a house with a sunroom or living room facing south and east, plus many other specific requests, just as we did for the motorhome. I included an east-facing master bedroom with deck, well-placed windows, away from highway noise, a garage, a large lot, and so many more impossible wants and desires. This was truly a faith list of all my extravagant hopes and dreams.

In childlike faith, I believed I needed to be specific and God would provide. The Lord showed me He loved it when I had such bold confidence in His goodness and ability to provide that I was willing to write down the details of my request and even the price I thought I could afford.

> Now to him who is able to do immeasurably more than all we ask or imagine, according to his power that is at work within us. (Ephesians 3:20)

The day after I wrote down my requests, my Realtor friend called me, saying, "There's this house that just came on the market, and it is in your price range." I drove to it on my lunch hour, saw it briefly, and immediately heard myself say, "I'll take it!" It was in Carbondale, not far down valley from Aspen.

It had every detail on my list! God is awesome! However, after I said I would take it, my Realtor said, "Well, there's no guarantee he will accept the offer." Although he wanted to get out of it quickly, the price was very low. My Realtor advised me that he might reject the figure, since he was not required to take it, and not to be surprised.

I said, "Why? I'm paying the full price!

She replied, "That's probably not enough."

However, when the owner's Realtor took my offer to him, he accepted it two days later! What a wonderful God moment that was.

The house had a sunroom that was not only south and east facing but also west, with a great view, a porch off the bedroom, and many places for plants. It was light and airy, scaled down in size, but very sound and had all the elements I asked for, including a modern kitchen with a dishwasher. It came with a clothes washer and dryer, a wood stove, and even a two-car garage. Although the final price was $19,000 more than on my list, the Lord provided the promotion that allowed the mortgage company to cover the gap! The whole church knew it as, "The house the Lord gave Bette." I knew it was all God.

When it became clear I was going to get the house, the people at church helped to connect me with Chandra, who wanted to share a house; she was a blessing. I was able to take most of her rent to reduce the principle on my mortgage before the first ARM increases. She was much younger than I was, and it gave me an opportunity to have a sense of family around me. We enjoyed inviting church friends to Sunday-afternoon dinners at the house.

Although grief and sorrow were always lurking in the shadows, I refused to look at the loss I felt and with the Lord's help put my focus back on Him. I lined up my Bible, concordance, and books on Wayne's side of the bed and would fall asleep at night memorizing Scriptures.

During this time, I surrounded myself with praise music. People would loan me a tape or make me a copy of theirs. I listened to constant praise while traveling in the car and at home. On weekends, I would work around the house just praising and singing to the Lord. I recognized and understood that He was right there with me. All these moments made this a time of celebration.

19. Moments of Comfort

I was very conscious I was single. I had no confidant beside me. I was lonely. If it had not been for the Lord, those months could have been devastating, but my renewed relationship with Him and His love truly made it a very good time.

> *to the One who remembered us in our low estate His love endures forever. (Psalm 136:23)*

During our separation, I ended up having three wonderful vacations. The first one was flying out to Pennsylvania for a wedding, where I made a significant reconnection with my extended family. Driving later with my parents to their home in North Carolina and spending a few days with them was comforting. Wayne drove over and picked me up since we agreed to spend one or two days dating and visit the Outer Banks. These were precious times with my relatives and with Wayne. When I flew home, I settled back into work and the church functions again.

The second one gave me an opportunity, with other church members, to go on a retreat in Colorado Springs. I rented a van and took people who did not have rides. There were four of us, and it was a precious and joyous time praising and singing to the Lord. The first stop was to visit Andrew Womack's church. At the end of the service, he invited people to come up for prayer. I asked that he pray for Wayne. He did and prophesied the following:

"The Lord says there are lots of things He wants to do concerning you and that husband. But first, the Lord says you need to change your focus. You need to put your attention back on the Lord. And there are certain things in your life that are going to have to run their course. It's going to take time for some things. Go to rejoicing in the Lord. As you start walking in that and rejoicing in Him, you're going to be a blessing to many people. While other people are saying, "Boy, you've got reasons to gripe and complain," I can see you walking in the joy of the Lord and being so thankful. Sister, the Lord says, "Just let it go." God's working on the husband. He's working on everything else. God will take care of you! Just go back to worshiping Him."

As I continued to switch my total focus from Wayne onto the Lord, it became a sweet time in the storm of separation.

Then I had a third vacation driving to Boise, Idaho, to visit our daughter, Theresa. I was able to spend a few wonderful days with her and Snowy the dog. I was normally too timid to undertake these opportunities on my own initiative. However, I learned to hold onto the Lord's strong hand, walk through the travel difficulties, and just enjoy these experiences. Each event was a precious personal God moment that encouraged my heart and kept me close to the Lord as I continued to focus on Him.

An intercessory prayer group at church that I was actively participating in met in the sanctuary once a week and we prayed for the church as a whole and for the needs of individual people. One night there were five of us praying when a young man walked through the front door looking for help. As we prayed for him, the Lord led me to share a Scripture:

> 'You are my servant'; I have chosen you and have not rejected you. So do not fear, for I am with you; do not be dismayed, for I am your God. I will strengthen you and help you; I will uphold you with my righteous right hand. (Isaiah 41:9b–10)

He broke down weeping and totally received this encouragement from the Lord. This greatly moved him, and it became a God moment for him. The Lord showed me that memorizing Scriptures is not just for me. In addition, we all chipped in and gave him gas money as he went on his way.

Lightning sparked historic forest fires in our area. This summer of our separation was unusually hot and dry. There was concern that the winds might carry embers from one mountaintop to another. This was a tense time for the entire neighborhood as the fires raged on for many days.

This was the fire season that took the precious lives of seven hotshot firefighters from Oregon. It was a time of mourning while we all waited for relief. I memorized and stood on this Scripture:

When you walk through the fire, you will not be burned; the flames will not set you ablaze. For I am the Lord your God, the Holy One of Israel, your Savior. (Isaiah 43:2b–3a)

Wayne and I remained in limited phone contact with each other during this time. Wayne let me know he was deciding whether or not to move to Atlanta. I needed him to know that I still loved him. I did not dare tell him what to do because I knew that would push him further away. I went to the pharmacy in town and found a card in the miscellaneous section. It did not say a lot, but I needed him to know that I still cared very much about him. I mailed it.

I was not comfortable with my Atlanta plans. While considering my future, I received the card from Bette. It was obviously God inspired, having words from our past that deeply touched me. Reading that card and the simple sentiment she wrote broke me up. My eyes flooded with tears. I decided to put out another fleece (see Judges 6:37–40) by writing two classified ads, one for my car and the other for the motorhome. I said out loud, so that God could hear, "If the car sells first, I will go to Atlanta. If the motorhome sells first, I will go back to Colorado." The motorhome sold the next day.

Upon arriving in Denver, I found a one-bedroom apartment in a high-rise building near the downtown mall. It was on the thirty-ninth floor, so I could see much of the city. I particularly liked the building lights at night. I always enjoyed upper floors from our times in large airport hotels, looking deeply over a city. I furnished my apartment sparsely but it was comfortable, and I enjoyed it very much. I found a job and settled into an acceptable routine. Later, when it was getting close to Thanksgiving, I bought a prepackaged dinner for two, figuring I would have one great meal and many leftovers. One afternoon I decided to phone Bette.

When he called me from Denver, I was overjoyed. I was at church helping serve an early Thanksgiving dinner to members and their friends.

In our conversation, we mentioned our lack of plans for the holiday. Bette said she did not have any food planned but asked cautiously if I would like to spend Thanksgiving with her. It sounded like a great idea, and besides, I had the food. I hurriedly got a bus ticket at the depot, which was closing just as I got there. I ran to catch the bus and had to bang on the door to stop it from leaving without me. It was a God moment when it all came together. I traveled up to Glenwood Springs, where Bette picked me up. Seeing her glowing smile made it seem as though I had never been away.

My housemate Chandra was in California with her family, so we had the house to ourselves. We were able to talk freely and share our thoughts and feelings like the best of friends. It soon became clear that we still loved each other deeply and wanted to be together again.

By the time I was to leave, we decided to reunite, provided I would stop drinking and get a job right away. Considering the limited job prospects in Aspen, it was a true God moment when a full-time bus-driving position opened up. I received this job over many applicants simply because I had experience driving a large motorhome. I met Bette's no alcohol requirement only through God's mercy, being able to stop cold turkey without any withdrawal symptoms. We drove to Denver, where I quit my job, arranged to give up the apartment, and loaded Bette's car with all my stuff. God was truly into the move because the management reluctantly agreed to let me out of my lease only when and if the apartment was re-rented. It only took a month.

We renewed our wedding vows in front of the whole church. I was giddy with anticipation, just like a new groom during the ceremony. Hope and excitement filled me.

Peace and joy overwhelmed me. It seemed as though we were married all over again! Our union was once again complete.

20. Tillamook, Oregon

Our life started over, with us enjoying each other's company as if nothing had ever happened. The house was great, my bus-driving job was going well, Bette's work was prosperous, and our times together seemed idyllic. We were lulled into a comfortable lifestyle, but bipolar was rising. I made several mania-induced errors in my driving, and at season's end, they did not ask me to return. I accepted this eventuality without a fight since I believed that somehow all would be well. After losing the bus job, I pursued other income-producing strategies, all to no avail. After these events passed, my mind switched into depression. Relentlessly, I beat myself up emotionally and once again convinced myself to flee from what looked like one more defeat.

After years of battling the oppressive atmosphere resulting from the nearly constant bipolar-fed emotional and financial battles in Aspen, I went for a long walk. Total discouragement flooded over me. I lost my will to fight. I was no longer interested in trying to make a go of it. As I walked, I found myself saying to the Lord, "I can no longer wear the mantle of meeting the needs of Your people and funding it by producing and selling a new product from an Aspen-based company." Instead of asking Him for help to continue in spite of my deepening frustrations, I asked for and received release from this work.

I immediately, and for the first time, felt completely separated from God. I found that I was alone and cold, and an empty feeling overwhelmed me. I knew the release happened; the awareness of it gave me both the freedom I asked for and the chilling knowledge that I just lost the Lord's perfect will for me.

I cried when Wayne told me what transpired between him and the Lord. I knew he was serious and had just closed the door on Aspen. After all our years of struggling financially, and throughout the separation, I was finally looking at defeat. I could not see an acceptable solution that would work for either my husband or myself. I knew for some time Wayne felt cornered. I understood his discouragement and came to realize we were not going to make it in Aspen.

I had refused to go on and turned my back on what the Lord gave me to do. The depth of what I just did shook me to my core. However, I did feel a great relief and soon found prayer to be easy again.

I started thinking about where to live next. During and after prayer times, I felt comfortable with the West Coast and especially the northwest states. I convinced Bette to take a night flight into Seattle.

At first, I was reluctant to scout out the land, but here we were on a night flight into Washington State. Seeing snow-covered volcanos below us in the bright moonlight made it all seem new and mysterious. I knew in my heart if we were with the Lord, anything would be possible. After driving around the Seattle and Portland areas, we found Oregon to be the most peaceable and desirable place.

In prayer back at home, the Lord reaffirmed His love and that it is fine with Him to need a new start. He wanted us to know that no love was lost between us. I once again felt comfortable around Him. In the quietness of my prayer times with the Lord, I knew we were now free to live anywhere.

After a great deal of prayer, we made preparations and forged ahead with plans to sell the Carbondale house, buy another motorhome with those proceeds, and make our way into the Pacific Northwest.

Ever since the vision, motorhomes always seemed to give us a sense of safety. Searching a large geographical area in a rig was easier to us than making trips by car and living out of suitcases; the familiarity of motorhomes was comfortable and freeing. Through many lengthy steps, the house finally sold and we packed up, this time into a large preowned motorhome.

While we were praying and looking over maps, the Lord guided us to check out some cities in Washington State. After our travels driving around Washington, through Walla Walla, other small communities, and Seattle, we became convinced we did not feel a sense of peace in that state and fully decided not to stay.

We found ourselves looking for a small town that was easy to live in and within driving distance to a large city. We decided to seek out a solid charismatic mega-church that we hoped would reenergize us to our original call, "Meet the needs of My people." We decided to drive down the coastal highway to see the ocean and search for a place to live. Our first stop was Cannon Beach, where we stayed for a week. We read signs near the beach talking about the dangers of sneaker waves and tsunamis, but their warnings seemed unreal. The town is clearly a tourist destination, and we were not looking for another Aspen-like town. It did not feel like home to us. We continued our travels down the Oregon coast.

Plowed sand and boats parked in front yards along the sides of the main road through town were the first things we saw when we arrived in Tillamook.

The TV revealed the monumental five hundred–year flood, sustained several months earlier, had hit them hard. We heard about the floods in Oregon when we were still in Colorado but did not make the connection to Tillamook until we arrived. Farmers lost entire herds of cattle, which was severe since the economy depends largely on the dairy industry. The main grocery store had sandbags piled up at the entrance. We found many businesses closed and boarded up. The town was clearly in a state of shock.

However, the community has a down-to-earth, wholesome family atmosphere. We felt a sense of peace and belonging just talking with some of the people. The climate is also comfortable as it is close to the ocean, plus the town is quaint, and the surrounding area is pleasant and pastoral.

Tillamook is close enough to Portland to make it all work, and we decided to make it our new home. We found a suitable RV park during our first few days and then embarked on finding a significant church in the greater Portland area.

We located New Beginnings church from the yellow pages and walked in on a world conference they were holding that whole week. We immediately found it a comfortable, godly refuge from the Aspen world we had just left. The events surrounding this time confirmed to us that we were once again following the Lord's gentle guidance. We wholeheartedly embraced this church and quickly became involved with their Freedom Tour. This outreach revival effort started in Seaside, Oregon, and concluded with a series of services in a large bull-fighting coliseum in Nogales, Mexico.

This new start to our life in Tillamook seemed fine, but the clouds of difficulty were not far away. The events about to happen were manic and then depressive. We hoped the medication Wayne was taking would work well enough in this new environment to control the swings in his moods.

Things started moving quickly during the next few months. We wanted to find a piece of bare land upon which we could park the motorhome. It needed to be available for our meager resources and to lend itself for building a house at some future date. We fell in love with a large piece of land for sale with a distant ocean view. After making several offers on it, we finally reached an agreement to buy it with an interest-only loan provided by the seller.

Wayne was eager to complete the deal but I had reservations over the terms. I supported him but now the manic side of his illness began to run its course. Wayne was taking his meds, but we still did not know they were ineffective. In spite of this, life seemed good.

Shortly after setting up on this land in the hills surrounding Tillamook, we purchased a satellite dish that was short one small piece not available locally. I received great support from Bette, who bought this part from a major RV supplier (four hours away) right as they were closing for the weekend. We successfully mounted the dish and receiver on the rig and gratefully received Trinity Broadcasting Network (TBN) Christian programs at two o'clock that Sunday morning.

Those first Praise the Lord *programs we received were highly Spirit filled, joyful, and triumphant revivals we soaked up every evening. Here we were dry camping on top of seventeen acres of backcountry woods, with no water or electricity, but watching quality Christian shows by generator power. We were basking in this glory-filled time with the Lord.*

We harvested rainwater from the motorhome awning, added some chlorine, and pumped it from a new fifty-five-gallon garbage pail with several filters to make the water safe to use. When it was not raining enough, the local water company allowed us to collect tap water from their outside faucet. We filled gallon bottles, poured them into our pail, and it worked just fine.

There were many beautiful moments on the land. On several nights, a rare bright comet lit up the darkened sky like a spotlight. On those few nights I ventured outside in the dark, the display of stars was glorious. The Lord's handiwork awed me.

One day I heard a great screeching sound up in the sky. When I stepped outside and looked up, I saw a huge bald eagle just sitting up high in a weathered tree. She calmly watched her eaglet, who was squawking furiously while being chased by a crow. I could imagine it calling out, "Ma! Ma! Do something!"

I found the hushed quiet that settled into the deep woods at night to be soothing and calming. I cherished this peaceful time and spent many blissful moments with the Lord.

We walked quietly along trails, where we saw clusters of little pink coastal flowers, wild bleeding heart, red columbine, foxglove, and holly berries. There was joy in watching a fawn that wandered into our little clearing to munch on blackberries. One day a migrating flock of woodpeckers swooped in and covered one of the trees as if they were looking for buried treasure. They were comical to watch for half an hour as they turned upside down to feast on insects. Then they flew off as a group, and I never saw them again.

In spite of all the beauty, I had an underlying fear we were going to run out of money before we succeeded.

I spent much time attempting to get electric power to the land and water from an underground spring. I even led us to design, and have a builder produce, house plans, anticipating we would build from revenues out of our newly formed company.

We started this small business upon settling in Tillamook. We based it on ideas created near the end of our time in Aspen when Wayne thought he might become a corporate speaker. We tried to acquire contracts to place motivational speakers into meetings and conferences for companies all over the country.

Our efforts included designing, producing, and mass mailing brochures. However, even with constant phone work and follow-ups, we only netted a few placements. Our best efforts in working for this company only resulted in much frustration and heartache. This self-designed business, created in mania and without much consultation with the Lord, predictably died.

Once again, the Lord showed that we did not find His best for us in our own thoughts and ideas but rather in consistently spending time with Him.

> *For the Lord gives wisdom, and from his mouth come knowledge and understanding. (Proverbs 2:6)*
>
> *Then you will understand what is right and just and fair-every good path. For wisdom will enter your heart, and knowledge will be pleasant to your soul. (Proverbs 2:9–10)*

Wayne fell into a deep depression, knowing we were falling short of success. We still did not understand that a bipolar depression usually followed his periods of manic activity.

We ended up losing the land, our motorhome, money, and the emotional stability we gained since moving to Tillamook as a result of bankruptcy.

It was a time of great sorrow and shame. Leaving the pristine countryside we loved so much was very disappointing, but it was time to regroup. We quickly needed jobs and a place to live.

21. He Heard Our Cry

We were out of resources and in constant prayer. The way the Lord answered these prayers was astounding and filled us with joy and the awareness that He was still right there with us. Just before we moved off the property, the Lord helped us find a short-term promotional job at the local Safeway store. They hired both of us for eight-hour days, and this filled the money gap for three weeks.

Along with this work, we hastily produced what we hoped would be acceptable resumes to answer a help-wanted ad for a property manager and maintenance team needed in Tillamook. The Lord was clearly involved with writing these resumes because the words flowed effortlessly onto the paper. We listed some of our skills in simple bullet points. It seemed the property supervisor received them as if the words held great power, giving us both positions quickly. As part of the package, this job even supplied housing. In addition, Safeway allowed total flexibility in our hours, so we were fully able to train for the new job the following week. The Lord amazingly created a godly victory by providing these answers to all our needs through His love and power, including dovetailing these two jobs together perfectly.

In spite of all our errors and wrong turns, the Lord did not give up on us.

Never will I leave you; never will I forsake you. (Hebrews 13:5b)

We were unwise, but His love was stronger than our weaknesses; His mercy and forgiveness covered our shame. While we were leaving the land, we could not believe we missed God again so completely, but the Lord embraced us without mentioning those times as He could have. He was and is our safe haven; God is awesome!

> *God is our refuge and strength, an ever-present help in trouble. (Psalm 46:1)*

Along with our ministering with the people of New Beginnings church, we found ourselves meeting the needs of young people and their parents at our new jobs. We were so grateful to be working in *Affordable Housing* because it seemed to be ideal for helping hurting people. At our first management site, Meadow Glen, there were kids all over the place. They had little to do and nowhere to go after school. We received authorization to build a playground and buy all new equipment. The Lord inspired me to gather the kids up and pore through catalogues with them as they picked out the pieces they liked; we planned the whole area together. It turned out to be the best one anywhere around and included a huge sand box with the typical slides, seesaws, jungle gym, swings, monkey bars, and more. After pouring the concrete half basketball court, we invited the kids to write their names and place handprints in the wet cement. The playground became a favorite gathering place for both kids and parents.

When it came time to clean up the property, we gave the youngsters bags and small latex gloves so they could help pick up trash and rewarded their efforts with peanuts and even nickels at one point. The parents approved of these treats, rather than sugary candy. We loved and appreciated our residents, and the Lord's compassion for them showed through us and created a strong bond between the residents and us. We considered it a privilege and found it easy to serve them with godly honor and respect.

We saw the Lord's favor and blessing in a powerful work of provision when the owner gave us management responsibility over an additional property in town. This one, called Sheridan Square, is for seniors or disabled residents. The Lord provided new housing at this position, and it gave us even better living conditions. The God-given desire to work with these additional residents provided many opportunities to serve in the work of low-income affordable housing management. This blessed work lasted for fourteen years.

22. The Last Bipolar, but Ouch!

During an original document review with my regional manager, we found that Sheridan Square was not required to provide on-site housing for the management team. Therefore, they asked us to find alternative living arrangements as soon as possible. The God moment was that this push out of our nest brought many things together. We had saved some money, the market for houses was good, and mortgage rates were low. Wayne's godly parents provided an inheritance that, along with everything else, helped us have enough money for a down payment.

I first started looking for a house within the city of Tillamook. One possibility was a beautiful remodeled house listed for more than we could afford. We made low offers for it and were in negotiations when another buyer came in and paid full price. We were deeply disappointed. Nevertheless, within a week or so Iris, the Realtor who worked with us on the first house, called me and offered to show a similar house if I wanted to see it. I was somewhat reluctant to try to find a house again so quickly, but it was only a block away from the first one. It also had three bedrooms with two and a half baths, which is unheard of in this area of town. Since Bette was working, Iris and I went to see it. I liked it right away. I called Bette and said, "I think we have found our house!" We went right over to look at it together. We were both excited, agreed this house looked very good and went home to look the listing over in detail. Everything continued to look great, especially the price. We made our plans with the Lord and closed the deal quickly.

We rejoice that we bought our home on Ivy Avenue and have constantly praised God for not letting us buy the first one; it was actually too large for us. This smaller Craftsman-style fully renovated house is extremely well done. It has two 1920s original high-quality wall heaters so it is easy to heat. It also has an attached garage that just fit our car bumper to bumper, and ample sunlight from many windows.

This house became a safe refuge from all of the medical challenges still ahead. One of these, the last major hospitalized bipolar event I have suffered, occurred shortly after we moved in.

The responsibility for finding a house, getting a mortgage, and working with the Realtors and salespeople fell primarily on Wayne since I continued to work long hours. This, and the pressures of the move, set him up for a relapse.

Before my hospitalization, even though I was making efforts to pray, a very subtle lie was being fed to my mind. I believed in excess that I was the all-powerful man of the house and needed to be fully in charge of everything. The weight of the move in concert with everything else led to this bipolar event.

It was easy for me to believe the constant lies of the Devil when I was weakened by mental illness and the simple duties of life.

When he lies he speaks his native language, for he is a liar and the father of lies. (John 8:44b)

It might have been obvious to me, had I not been so sick, that my responses to the pressures of the move were nothing less than spiritual battles going on with Satan.

> *Be self-controlled, and alert. Your enemy the devil prowls around like a roaring lion, looking for someone to devour. (1 Peter 5:8)*

It started during the move and continued for three and a half months where Wayne was showing the effects of bipolar mania, including antagonism and arrogance toward me in all of our daily encounters. He also said he felt the house was his and even threatened to lock me out.

I was taking my meds only sporadically, actually absentmindedly, without telling Bette, and then I quickly spiraled into mania. I angrily knocked all my open medication bottles off a table and spilled the pills out and onto the floor. I then threw furniture, lamps, and kitchen stuff all around the house; I frightened Bette a great deal.

The morning that everything escalated, I heard the Lord clearly: "Do not stand in his way." I knew Wayne did not want to go to a hospital, but after the bipolar illness swung wildly, it became evident that I needed to get more help for him than I could do at home.

His psychiatrist told me to call 911 if it continued or became worse. Wayne went all the way from rage to a catatonic state. He would not take the meds his psychiatrist told me to give him. I thank the Lord that when I could not take care of him myself, God opened a door to get him the care he needed. I called 911, and when the ambulance and a police officer arrived, they took charge, strapped Wayne to a gurney, and took him away. I asked if I should follow in my car, but they said it wasn't necessary because the local hospital would not let me see him anyway. After a short lockdown, they transported him to another facility.

While dealing with the severity of this attack, Bette was seeing a doctor about having chronic exhaustion. This became very serious while I was in the psychiatric hospital for a month and a half.

This was a difficult period because the stresses of the last months had taken their physical toll and left me helpless. It was impossible to do anything more than go to work and deal with the medical crises as they came up. The difficulties seemed like they would never end. I felt such deep sorrow that I was numb.

My time became very difficult. I was making outlandish bipolar manic demands on Bette to buy a classic Mercedes and could not understand her resistance to my requests. She would not do what I wanted and just immediately countered with, "We really can't afford it."

The charge nurse recommended that I stop communicating with Wayne by phone because he got worse after talking with me. As a result, the lack of contact separated us, and we both felt rejected.

These feelings were intense and did start to divide and isolate us from each other. We both began to feel as if the other one stopped caring.

I would still try to reach the head nurse every night, but she was seldom available. When I asked other nurses about his condition, they always replied, "You will have to get that information from her." It was a difficult time of separation.
Because of this and the way I was feeling physically, I would come home from work at night and go

right to bed. I lost my focus on the Lord, and waves of discouragement buffeted me. The deep exhaustion I was feeling really became debilitating for me six months after Wayne's hospitalization. It was so bad I could not even walk from my desk to the restroom. It forced me to go on medical leave.

While at home, the two of us began telling each other about our hurts and frustrations during the hospitalization.

A legal requirement stipulated that I could not leave Tillamook for at least six months in order to stay out of the hospital and not be recommitted. Follow-up visits were required weekly, and sometimes more often, with my caseworker and my psychiatrist. I also had to put the house back together as it was and do a number of other repair jobs left undone from the move.

Actually, I believe the hospital let me out too early. When I got home, the effects of bipolar were still with me, and I continued to think that Bette had had enough of me and wanted out of the relationship. I answered those feelings by distancing myself from her both physically and emotionally. I was seriously thinking of leaving her again and starting over with a female doctor I had grown attached to at the hospital. I moved out of the house and lived in our small motorhome on the side yard for several months.

When I turned my attention back on the Lord, He lovingly protected me from any negative thoughts about this situation. As I was praying, I found myself wanting to find a way to reach out to Wayne and do something loving and kind. I received the thought of going to a shop forty-five minutes away in Cannon Beach to look for the right kind of string needed to fly his stunt kite. I offered and Wayne accepted a motorhome trip to do this in early March.

Midway through our trip, a damaged storage door kept flying open. It would not close. I knew it could tear off the rig easily, but we were on the road and halfway to our destination when it happened. I put out another fleece, saying to the Lord silently that if He could keep it attached all the way up and back home then I would stay and try to work things out with Bette. However, if it opened farther and became a real road hazard, I would be free to leave. I was sure it would blow off but it stayed connected, as if a wind was blowing it closed. I could not deny this obvious God moment, but I waited until we arrived home to tell Bette what happened.

When Wayne first shared this with me, I did not fully understand the significance of this moment to him and that the Lord convinced him to stay permanently. Wayne truly made up his mind that day. Thank You, Jesus.

I continue to be grateful that Bette accepted me moving back into the house and even for us to sleep in the same bed. Nevertheless, once again, we found there was much work to do on our marriage.

It took time but in spite of all this sorrow, and the complicated feelings we had toward each other, the Lord began the healing process for each of us. Three months later, when my physical exhaustion forced the medical leave, it gave us time to stop and hear each other while we talked things out. All of our lives we have always been strong when we are together. Nevertheless, if it had not been for the Lord, the Devil could have succeeded in destroying Wayne's life and our marriage. However, the Lord's power overcame everything thrown at us and kept us safe in His love.

Love is patient, love is kind. It does not envy, it does not boast, it is not proud. It is not rude, it is not self-seeking, it is not easily angered, it keeps no record of wrongs. Love does not delight in evil but rejoices with the truth. It always protects, always trusts, always hopes, always perseveres. Love never fails. (1 Corinthians 13:4–8a)

23. Tying It All Together

I see how often I did not obey Him quickly and completely but put my focus onto just living life and dealing with bipolar symptoms. Unfortunately, disobedience has been a common thread in my relationship with the Lord.

However, the Lord shows His character by being willing to forgive and be patient with me. Proof of this is in my current journals, where He speaks about enjoying our times together simply because I come back to Him in quiet prayer times. In addition, He has blessed and refreshed me by calling us to action once more. We may be able to share this new journey with Him in a subsequent book. Time will tell.

I am continuing my growth with the Lord, leaning on His Word and receiving His love. I am grateful for the Lord's faithfulness by revealing promises in His Word when I need them and protecting and helping me at every turn in my life. I am amazed at how many times He was right next to me. Because He never changes, believing the promises He made in the Old and New Testaments makes me stand strong today. Psalm 91 is one of my favorites. It promises if I live in the shelter of the most high God, I do not have to fear anything.

As I ask the Lord for forgiveness from all of my specific errors, I found myself greatly freed from my emotional burdens. When I got authentic with God the Father, His Son Jesus, and the Holy Spirit, I found many God moments and now have a close relationship with the Maker of them. I am now able to communicate with my heavenly Father, be totally at peace, and read His Word with confidence and ease. When I go to the Father in prayer, I have a sense of awe and anticipation, knowing He will be right there with me and willing to talk. Finding the Lord and experiencing His loving touches was definitely worth the effort.

> *let us draw near to God with a sincere heart in full assurance of faith, (Hebrews 10:22a)*

Concerning bipolar, Bette prayed that the Lord's will would be done and that every meeting would be valuable before I went to each appointment with my new psychiatrist. After she did, I had a peace that God would indeed open a door to my full healing. Significant medication changes and adjustments contributed to the success of these endeavors and provided one huge God moment for us when I finally became consistently better on three meds taken together.

I also received much counseling all along this journey. Medicine and professionals helped but not alone. I recognized God's personal involvement in becoming the foundation for my healing, but even after seeing so many miracles happen around me, I had trouble believing for my own until Bette prayed.

A few meds prescribed by a previous doctor started to help Wayne, but the side effects were intolerable. I noticed that the Lord provided a safety net of peace around him that lessened his uneasiness during all the changes.

My current condition is total remission from the disabling scourge of bipolar disorder. The release from its mental pressure has removed the nearly constant feelings of manic edginess or impending doom. I am thrilled to be at this point in my healing. My peace and enjoyment of life are remarkable since I am now sane and sober. At this time, the healing has lasted over six years.

I am profoundly grateful not only to be alive but also to experience peace, joy, and a newfound sense of living at ease. I am now comfortable in my skin.

The Lord protected Wayne many times over. I praise God that we both survived.

> *No temptation has seized you except what is common to man. And God is faithful; he will not let you be tempted beyond what you can bear. But when you are tempted, he will also provide a way out so that you can stand up under it. (1 Corinthians 10:13)*

> *because of the Lord's great love we are not consumed, for His compassions never fail. They are new every morning; great is your faithfulness.(Lamentations 3:22–23)*

For me, bipolar of the past is like a bad dream that fades in the morning sunshine. Today my anticipation of the future is full of hope. My prospects look brighter than I ever imagined, and I'm thrilled to be at the side of my sane husband. Wayne's present-day peace is contagious, and I am grateful the Lord made this possible.

Bette and I are relishing our time together since I feel and act normal every day. Today, as we sit peacefully side by side, I recognize how intimately God has been involved in our lives. My relationship with Bette is flourishing due to her love and undying faithfulness to me. I am growing deeper in love with her more each day. I am such a fortunate man.

I am so grateful the Lord God was an everlasting help in each crisis and actually continues now in every part of our life. Wayne's refreshing and newly rekindled kindness, gentleness, and tenderness toward me mean everything. It's almost like dating and falling in love all over again. I have all the elements of romance filling my every desire; our love is deep and sincere. It is hard to look back because today is so wonderful. It feels like a beginning, not an end to this story.

I view the motorhome as a tool the Lord used to test and grow our obedience and faith. I now see it was a kindness of the Lord to give us a sense of home for our family while moving us from an entrenched position in Connecticut. Prior to the vision, we never considered living anywhere else. Embracing the call to sell everything, including our home, seemed like a giant step. It did not occur to me it was just the first one.

I found motorhome life exciting and challenging. Following the Lord seemed like it would be easy. However, in spite of the vision and its realization, we did not convert the motorhome into full-time use simply by neglecting what the Lord specifically directed me to do. I was in a state of shock when I reread a journal entry written a few years after buying our rig.

The Lord said:

> I want you to travel freely over the next several years. You need to know the people you are going to serve. I have told you this before.

I asked the Lord, "What people will we be serving? Church attendees? Jews? Gentiles? Who do we need to know about?"

> You need to know the needs of all My people. I want you to go and find out what My people think their needs are. All of My people have needs, but they think their needs are different from what they truly are.
>
> Then I want you to read My Word and find out what I see as the needs of My people. A great gulf exists between what I see and what they see. Your role in the future is to bridge the gap between these two ways of looking at the same situation so I can meet their true needs and My people can receive My blessing.

I asked, "How do we find out what their needs are?"

> Ask them. Go from place to place and learn about My people and learn about Me. As I told you before, this is absolutely necessary in order for you to serve. You are free to go wherever you care to go, to learn about My people. Where you go and how you respond to this call will determine, in part, how you will serve.

From my current perspective, it seems impossible that I could have so completely missed this entry concerning traveling rather than settling, but I did. I found it tucked in between other "more pressing" entries and blindly skipped over it. Nevertheless, His mercy and forgiveness continue to flood me with peace over this issue.

I see the Lord dealing with me much like my GPS. No matter if I take a wrong turn, thinking I see a shortcut, it always recalculates from where I end up and still leads me to my desired destination. Although it often takes backtracking and some extra time, I never get totally lost when I look to Him.

We had childlike faith while we were still in Connecticut. We had godly blessings and a wonderful time at PTL, and we know it was a firm call from the Lord to go to Aspen. However, we were not ready for, or able to handle, the bipolar, spiritual battles, and emotional stresses we encountered in Aspen, Colorado. Nevertheless, God filled our time in the Aspen area with outstanding moments, notwithstanding the defeats surrounding completing the product project under the throes of bipolar. The beautiful village, billowing snow, and sunny days with crisp nights all worked together to make it very desirable to us. The Lord provided repeated housing miracles, led the creation of an unknown product, caused miraculous healings, and blessed us with significant protection.

Even with these experiences and the knowledge of the Lord we took to Aspen, we needed much more. Knowing the Lord, and experiencing just some of what He can do, was not enough to support victorious Christian living in this difficult situation. We needed a lot more spiritual strength than we possessed at that time. Although there were many victories in Aspen, our overwhelming feelings were that we did not have the strength to keep going. We slowly withered.

We are very comfortable with our life and location now, but the Lord, over the last year and a half, has made it clear that Aspen and the product are still on the table. However, He has made a steep requirement that we must meet before this can become a reality.

Many battles have been fought to gain control of the lands God gave His people. The Israelites have returned to their promised land. Now, His leading is for us to consider reclaiming our promised land. It seems beyond our reach, as things have been all through our journey with God. However, I believe we will once again call Aspen, home.

Appendix 1. Housing

The faith required to have good housing always seemed to be strong in us, and the Lord has used that faith to give us many moments of victory.

Our heart has always been to do the will of the Lord and not just to find decent places to live. Nevertheless, He has always improved our housing situation as we found and stood on this Scripture:

> *Peter said to him, "We have left all we had to follow you!" "I tell you the truth," Jesus said to them, "no one has left home or wife or brothers or parents or children for the sake of the kingdom of God will fail to receive many times as much in this age and, in the age to come, eternal life." (Luke 18:28–30)*

This is one we have believed and relied upon from the very beginning of our walk. As we look back over the years, we have received this promised housing reward many times over.

When we left our house in Connecticut and entered the motorhome, we basked in those incredible housing moments with great gratitude. When we left the motorhome to live in Aspen the second time, we rejoiced at being downtown with a spectacular view of Aspen Mountain in a beautiful two-bedroom, two-bath apartment. Every time we moved, we saw it as an improvement. We rented a three-bedroom house in a premier location in Aspen's West End. Then we were able to purchase a three-bedroom, two-bath house with views and sun in Old Snowmass. Again, we rejoiced in the way it came about, giving the honor to the Lord. When Wayne left me, the Lord answered my needs with the purchase of a three-bedroom, one-and-a-half-bath house with sunroom and views again.

After we reunited and drove away from Aspen, it was in a preowned, high-end motorhome that took us to Tillamook. We traded up to another motorhome when we needed a much stronger engine to climb up the hill onto the land. Again, the Lord blessed us with God moments time after time.

It was our simple, unshakable belief that God's Word is true that allowed His power to bless us in this area. When it came time to leave the land, we received the blessing of a large, three-bedroom, one-bath apartment right where we worked. When a promotion to two properties occurred, we rejoiced in a brand-new two-bedroom, two-bath apartment in a quiet senior setting. Now we are in retirement, and as of this writing, the Lord has blessed us by allowing us to own a beautiful two-story, three-bedroom, two-and-a-half-bath home on a quiet road in downtown Tillamook.

In this one area, we have learned to do things God's way by believing and acting in full confidence on His promises in the Word. However, in other areas we are still working with the Lord, continuing to grow in faith and seeking His ways.

Appendix 2. Healings

Healing 1

We were new at believing and had just begun experiencing God's power. Wayne discovered a new hard bump, the size of a small pea, on the back of his hand. We thought he might need medical help to find out what was going on.

However, while watching a Christian TV program, they prayed specifically for healing. I had an assurance that the gift of faith was strong in me, and I accepted that prayer as mine. Whether the faith came from inside me or directly from the Spirit of God, I do not know. I do know it came from a position of peace and confidence. The bump went down instantly and never returned.

When I came home from work and heard about this event, I rejoiced in the Lord and declared, "Oh! Praise You, Father!" Wayne kept checking his hand, but it really was gone. It proved to us that God cares, even for the little things that disturbed our peace.

Excitement filled our days because we were seeing supernatural occurrences. We were in a state of high expectation simply because we were so intent on what He might do.

Healing 2

While we were living with Wayne's parents, we decided to look for a born-again church. After finding one in the newspaper, we made a trip down into Danbury, Connecticut, the following Sunday morning to attend a small church service. On that particular morning, the pastor was teaching on healing and the prayer of faith. At the end of the service, he told us, "Stand up and touch the part of your body where you are expecting a healing."

I had a diagnosis of psoriasis pustules and suffered with it for many years; it was like chronic poison ivy. When the pastor prayed, I believed this was my time for healing, and I prayed with him. Within a week, the skin became normal again on my fingers. Later on when the symptoms started up again, I rebuked them, resisted them, and declared, "The prayer of faith has gone up." After making this declaration, I went about my business, and the next day the skin was normal again. This healing God moment has lasted over thirty-five years!

Healing 3

A need for healing existed because I had severe migraines ever since my teenage years. I dealt with them for such a long time, and even at our wedding reception, I was so sick I could not leave the hotel bathroom.

The Christian campground of PTL was holding a big Labor Day event that included the healing ministry of Oral Roberts. They scheduled him to speak at the large auditorium called "the barn." They asked us to give up our campsite to make room for the expected crowds. This meant we would be in an undeveloped area with no electricity.

With so many people around, we were not at ease running our noisy generator. Without air conditioning, it was stifling, with the air being very hot and still. I suddenly had a headache I thought I could overcome. However, it accelerated to the point where my vision was affected, and I quickly deteriorated into the full cycle of pain. I came to the point where I could not stand light. The pain was so debilitating that nothing made sense. I was so sick that all I could do was lie on the sofa and try to keep from throwing up.

Wayne was getting ready to go into work. There was no way I could get up, go through the crowds, and attend that healing service. This is where Wayne's righteous anger and faith rose up.

I was hoping she could go have Oral Roberts pray for her, but I agreed with Bette that she was far too sick to go. However, her not being able to receive prayer frustrated and angered me. Then it hit me; I have just as much faith as Oral Roberts. Besides, I knew God was the same God where we were in the motorhome as at the service. I decided to ask the Lord for Bette's healing according to His Word:

> *Until now you have asked for nothing in my name. Ask and you will receive, and your joy will be complete. (John 16:24)*

I was also leaning on our experience with the healing of our daughter Wendy, which we talked about in chapter 1. I laid my hands on Bette and prayed against the migraine that hit her so hard. I asked for healing to be done in Jesus' name.

I left for work and heard nothing more about it. I just knew she was extremely uncomfortable.

I rested a little bit after his prayer. I also received this touch as from God because when Wayne spoke the prayer, he also said the words, "It's Jesus doing the healing, and that same Jesus is here." I simply believed. My complete healing occurred that afternoon, and I have never had that sickening migraine pain ever again. What an incredible God moment that truly was. After many years of suffering, it was amazing to be free, and I knew the Lord had done it. I praise God those headaches are in the past, now for over thirty-five years!

Healing 4

Another type of healing came after I procrastinated getting a mammogram for a very long time. The Lord nudged me just to get it done. I made an appointment right away before I could delay again. The test revealed a lump that had just started to grow, and soon thereafter, I received the diagnosis of breast cancer. I thank the Lord it was found so early that even after the location of it showed up on the mammogram, neither the doctor nor I could feel it. I know in my heart that if it had not been for God, the cancer would have had time to spread. After a simple lumpectomy and a short-term, high-dose radiation treatment, I was completely healed and I have been cancer free for nine years! We also thank the Lord for the fairly new (at that time) rapid treatment plan because we were four hours, round trip, away from the hospital, and the daily treatment was shortened to a matter of weeks rather than months.

Healing 5

Then a healing occurred during a time of severe exhaustion. One doctor, an endocrinologist, was about to leave the examination room at the end of the appointment when she turned and said, "Let me just check your heart." I firmly believe the Lord must have prompted her to do this. When she checked me, a very loud heart murmur became obvious. It was so alarming that she called our family doctor with the strong recommendation that I see a cardiologist as soon as possible. I was seeing other specialists at that time, but none of them had sounded an alarm.

When the cardiologist heard the murmur, it didn't seem to be a matter of extreme urgency to him.

However, on a follow-up visit, all of my fingers turned dark blue. This had never happened before. The Lord prompted Wayne to press for further tests. A scheduled echocardiogram revealed definite heart valve leakage. After more tests and procedures showing serious valve malfunction, they finally scheduled me for open-heart surgery.

After two operations on successive days, Bette ended up with a pair of mechanical heart valves and a pacemaker. Afterward the surgeon said to me, "You are a very fortunate man. It's a good thing you came when you did because the valves were so calcified and leaky, she almost had a massive heart attack right on the table."

The heart itself was normal and beating just fine, but the doctor found severely damaged valves. We got there just in time. We have seen this "just in time" type of moment happen many times over. I recognize that having a "knowing," an awareness, and the nudge to do something and to do it when there is no time to spare are actually very special God moments.

Healing 6

About a year later, Bette was having great difficulty with severe headaches, constant nausea, and some unsteadiness in walking. This went on for about two weeks, with the doctor prescribing meds for what he believed was the flu. It was not.

I woke up one morning with a vivid black and blue lower lip and still had a horrible headache. This alerted us to call the doctor, who sent me over to the lab to check my blood thinner level and then quickly to the emergency room to get a CAT scan of my head.

They allowed me to watch the monitor as the tests were going on, and I could clearly see a large white area showing up on the front and side of her brain. They took another scan showing more detail, and it showed the same thing. The ER doctor quickly reversed her blood thinner level. They informed us she was going by ambulance to the neurosurgery department of a Portland hospital because she suffered a hemorrhagic stroke; there was a pool of blood on her brain. I overheard discussions saying that if the lip had not happened, the possible delay in treatment could have allowed a debilitating stroke.

After the ambulance left, I went home and called our friends, who allowed the Lord to work quickly through them to bring help as she cared for our cats and watched over the house in our absence. I hastily threw some things into a suitcase and made the arduous trip through blinding rain, at night and with uncertain directions, to a hospital more than two hours away. I prayed in earnest for safety on the entire trip since Bette was the better driver of the two of us. The Lord provided a cocoon of peace around me during the whole trip.

A radiology technician friend told me later that people who have blood on their brains often end up with major disabilities, and some don't make it at all. Therefore, he was very concerned about us when he found out why we were going to Portland. He and his wife prayed for us, and they called other precious friends, who also prayed.

It really made the difference because I spent eight days in the hospital without surgery and without any further complications. Praise God! The blood completely reabsorbed into my body within just a few months. This was our first stroke miracle God moment.

Healing 7

Then it happened again a few months later: Bette woke up and could not speak clearly. One side of her mouth was drawn up and the other side drooping.

Before going to the emergency room, we prayed together. I also wanted Wayne to call Joel Osteen's TV ministry for prayer. In my heart, I wanted to go to the Lord first before going to the doctors.

By the time we were able to get a CAT scan, nothing showed up and her slurred speech kept improving. However, the neurosurgeon at the hospital in Portland wanted us there in case something new was happening in her brain. An ambulance took her to OHSU hospital for the second time.

Praise the Lord, when the doctors checked me out, none of them could find anything wrong. I know God healed me.

They released her the next day, saying there was no stroke, there was no need for another MRI, and all tests were normal. Once again, the power of God was amply apparent.

And now, if we may, we would like to pray with you:

> *Holy Father, we ask you to come into the reader's mind and heart, and to reveal Yourself fully to them. And we thank You that Your power will provide for their needs. May they receive all that You have for them. Thank You Lord for blessing them mightily!*
>
> *Amen.*

Thank you for reading!

We hope you enjoyed *God Moment: Hearing God's Voice Sparks a Remarkable Experience*. We really love sharing events involving the Lord.

As authors, we love feedback. Actually, you're the reason we've shared our experiences. Tell us what you liked, what you loved, or even what you didn't like. We'd love to hear from you and to share in your God moment experiences. You can write us at godmomenthearinggodsvoice@gmail.com

Finally, we need to ask a favor. If you're so inclined, we'd love a review of *God Moment*. Whether you loved it or not so much—we'd just enjoy your feedback. Reviews can be tough to come by these days, and you, the reader, have the power to make or break a book. If you have the time, here's how to find our review page: On *Amazon Books*, search *God Moment Bette and Wayne Price*, then click on our book.

Thank you so much for reading, spending time with us, and sharing.

Bette and Wayne

Made in the USA
San Bernardino, CA
21 February 2016